A BUMPY RIDE

A BUMPY RIDE

ONE HUNDRED AND FIFTY YEARS
OF HADEN MANUFACTURING
IN THE WEST MIDLANDS

DONALD HADEN

ALSO WITH CHAPTERS BY
PETER AND SALLY HADEN

A Bumpy Ride
Donald Haden

Published by Aspect Design 2015
Malvern, Worcestershire, United Kingdom.

Designed, printed and bound by Aspect Design
89 Newtown Road, Malvern, Worcs. WR14 1PD
United Kingdom
Tel: 01684 561567
E-mail: allan@aspect-design.net
Website: www.aspect-design.net

ISBN 978-1-908832-84-9

CONTENTS

ACKNOWLEDGEMENTS

First of all I should like to warmly thank the staff at Birmingham Reference Library who have always been most helpful. Also I am grateful for having been allowed to draw on information from the Vintage-Cycle Club library, the Herbert Synyer Archives and the archives of the National Cycle Museum in Llandrindod Wells. The National Motorcycle Museum in Birmingham has preserved, on public display, a magnificent example of an early Haden New Comet motorcycle and this is very much appreciated.

With gratitude I acknowledge Roger Dodsworth of Broadfield House Glass Museum in Stourbridge for not only helping my sister search for Haden ancestors in British glassmaking, but also for introducing us to Akiko Inoue Osumi, a Japanese glass historian, who together with Ritsuo Yoshioka of the Japan Uranium Glass Collectors Club has given invaluable information on the business activities of a Scottish member of our family who lived in Japan during the latter part of the nineteenth century.

Thanks are also due to my second cousin David Haden and to Stephanie Gore and Annette Payne for their excellent illustrations. Tess Lawley-Wakelin and her family have given much appreciated advice on certain family business matters in the immediate post-war period and I would like to thank friends still engaged in the bicycle trade for their valuable perspectives on past events and their encouragement to keep going on what has proved to be a far bigger project than was at first envisaged. Finally, I must record tremendous thanks to my sister, Sally; my twin brother, Peter; and my cousin John for their very useful contributions, and to my Jack Russell terrier, Tommy, who has encouraged me to go walking in the open countryside whenever he has seen me at my computer looking exhausted and in need of some fresh air.

Donald Haden with Tommy.

PREFACE

History is not the study of the past,
but of the surviving traces of the past.

(A truism of unknown origin)

It must have been in 1966 when, sitting in my office in the newly extended first floor of our Birmingham Westley Street factory, there was a knock on the door and in walked Jack Slater, our welding shop foreman, carrying a large dusty parcel wrapped in brown paper and tied up with string. The parcel was partly torn open and I could see that the contents appeared to be a large number of old photographs. At that time we were in the process of reorganising the layout of several areas of the factory and this included clearing out the old offices at the rear of the premises that had been closed up for twelve years.

The photographs had been discovered under the wooden floor of what had been, until 1953, my father's office. How or why they ever came to be there was never clear, but they were almost certainly in the same original wrapping, having probably been parcelled up at the time of the move in 1938 from what had been my grandfather's factory in Princip Street in the Birmingham Gun Quarter.

For reasons none of my generation within the family understood, my father had always been very reluctant to talk about the past. This was perhaps because he did not want to remind himself of the painful period just before the war when it was a struggle to keep the business going and relationships within the family were difficult. These photographs were, therefore, to me a goldmine of information about the family's industrial past, including pictures of not only my grandfather Alfred Haden who passed away shortly before I was born, but also my great grandfather George Haden, who was said to have started the business in 1869. Such was the all pervading secrecy within the family that I had never seen any photographs of this kind before, and digging deeper into the parcel I found a treasure trove of pictures of motorcycles and motorcycle parts that appeared to have been manufactured by my grandfather in the period between 1903 and 1931.

Clearly there was an interesting story to be told, but my father remained reluctant to expand on the limited information we had, and it was not until after I retired in 2002 that I found the time, and indeed felt—with the encouragement of other members of the family—the real need to place on record what is, I believe, an interesting example of how a family business could survive many difficulties, which were often outside its own control, and be passed down through several generations.

Although we can trace the family back to the early eighteenth century, the oldest positive record we have been able to find of a Haden business comes from a lease dated 1859 lodged in the Black Country Museum archives. This refers to a partnership between master glass cutters James Parrish, Joseph Lowe and William Haden who were setting themselves up in a workshop in Wordsley in the Black Country. William was my great-great-grandfather. From that date we have been able to trace a continuous line of Haden family businesses that have been freshly started or handed down from father to son for more than one hundred and fifty years.

There can be no doubt that the period of motorcycle manufacture is one of the more interesting parts of this history, but I felt in writing this book that it was important to place that in the context of events before and after and so, while many of the photographs from the old brown parcel are now contained within this book, I have been able to add more contemporary notes and pictures from my own records as well as information on nineteenth-century activities.

Additionally, I have come to appreciate the importance of later family enterprises: the valuable contributions of my twin brother, Peter, who, with his wife, Moira, built up a prominent and much-respected hotel business on the west coast of Ireland; and my cousin John, who took over the reins from his father of a major domestic appliance business they had created in Staffordshire, following an earlier start in Birmingham. These are therefore included.

This book would not have been possible without the tremendous help, encouragement and expertise of my sister, Sally Haden, who has not only written the important chapter relating to the family's early involvement in the glass industry, but has been particularly responsible for a great deal of original research work. Between us, we have been determined to make this, as far as is possible, a truly accurate record and, we hope, at the same time an interesting read.

Additional information on the history of our industrial past can be found on our website: www.hadenheritage.co.uk

DPH, 2015.

PROLOGUE

In his excellent book *Velocipedes, Bicycles and Tricycles—How to Make and How to Use Them* the author Velox, after first acknowledging the French as the prime movers in bicycle development, describes the scene in 1869 as follows:

> At the beginning of January it was estimated that there were in New York and its immediate vicinity alone no less than 5,000 persons who either knew how to ride the velocipede or were learning, and it was estimated that at least half that number would be mounted during the summer . . . In England we are supposed to be a sensible people, neither affecting the excitement of the French or the sensationalism of the Americans, yet in the matter of velocipedes we have indulged in some strange vagaries . . . Manchester has caught the fever, Birmingham has the symptoms. London is talking over the new excitement. The watering-places are thankful for the new sensation . . .

Velocipedes were, of course, a very primitive form of bicycle propelled either by the riders' legs pushing alternately against the ground or, as later developed, by peddling directly a crank mechanism attached to the front wheel. The development of the 'high bicycle',

Riding school, Broadway, New York, (where the fees were $15 per month).

commonly known as a penny-farthing or ordinary, enabled a greater speed to be achieved and these were no doubt of great interest at the time, and a source of fun and enjoyment, if not in any sense a practical means of regular transport. It was not until the introduction of the Rover Safety bicycle in 1885, with its chain drive to the rear wheels, followed soon after with the application of Dunlop pneumatic tyres, that the bicycle became a means of transport for all to ride. What was so significant about the chain driven bicycle was that average journey speeds of about 10 m.p.h. could now be easily achieved, compared to 3 m.p.h. for walking and 6 m.p.h. on a trotting horse. Those with no other means of transport could now substantially increase their circle of friends, their job opportunities and their social activities.

The subsequent development of the petrol engine, used first in automobiles towards the end of the century, offered the opportunity for a more exciting means of propulsion. It was the appearance, in about 1902, of a smaller, lighter engine, which could be fitted in the centre of the bicycle, driving the rear wheel by a belt or chain, that enabled two-wheeled bicycles to be motorised. From this basic design the motorcycle industry emerged, providing a new and more advanced means of travel.

Meanwhile, the development of the motor car continued apace—although in the early days these were primarily for the wealthy classes—and tractors and lorries were in great demand. In Birmingham in 1910, Herbert Austin produced the first British-made small family car and although production levels by 1914 had only reached thirty cars per week, the car was re-launched in 1922 as the Austin 7 and soon outsold all its rivals.

It was only natural, following earlier production in Wolverhampton and Coventry, that Birmingham—the city of a thousand trades—with its highly skilled and flexible workforce, should be the cradle for the development of these important industries and it was at the age of eighteen in 1869 that George Haden, the son of a glass cutter from Wordsley, is believed to have first became involved in the exciting world of bicycle racing and manufacture.

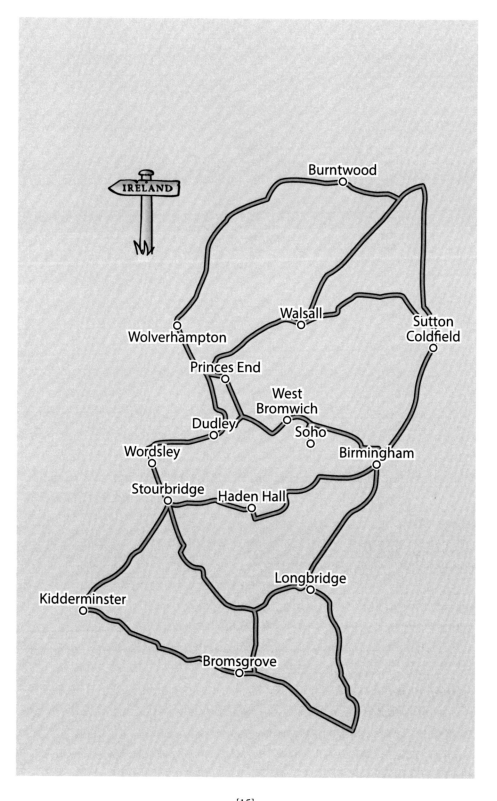

From a lease dated 14 May 1859

ORIGINS OF THE FAMILY NAME

The earliest trace of the use of the name Haden in the area that was to become known as the Black Country comes from the records of a family bearing that name, who lived for more than eight hundred years in Rowley Regis, about two miles south of Dudley. Ricardo Haden, a minor noble who supported William the Conqueror, built a small fortress to defend his landholding. Succeeding generations increased the size of the estate, building a more comfortable new home in 1310 that became known as Haden Hall.

Although during the twentieth century the family name Haden spread out across the West Midlands and the rest of the United Kingdom and elsewhere, population surveys show that in the Victorian period the greatest concentration of families bearing the name Haden was in the Black Country around Dudley, said to be the epicentre of the Industrial Revolution.

There have been several businesses established in the West Midlands over the past two hundred years bearing the Haden family name and it is important in reading this book to note, therefore, that it is only those established first by William Hamlet Haden (1821–1866), his direct descendants and those emanating from the second marriage of his grandson Alfred Hamlet Haden (1875–1940) and their descendants that have been included.

The Principal Haden Male Line of Descent

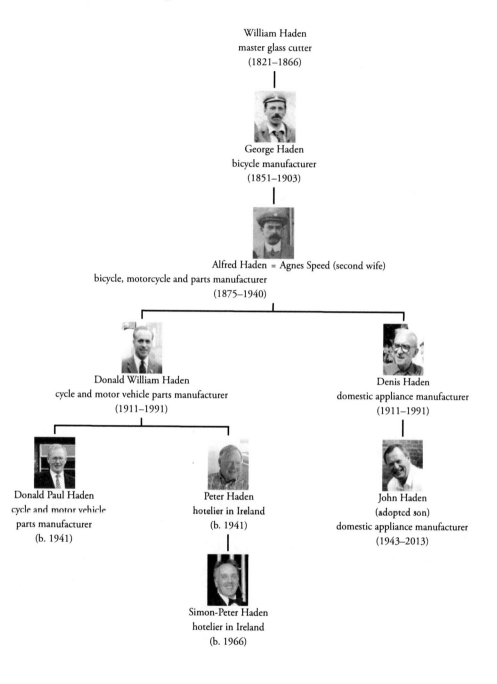

William Haden
master glass cutter
(1821–1866)

George Haden
bicycle manufacturer
(1851–1903)

Alfred Haden = Agnes Speed (second wife)
bicycle, motorcycle and parts manufacturer
(1875–1940)

Donald William Haden
cycle and motor vehicle parts manufacturer
(1911–1991)

Denis Haden
domestic appliance manufacturer
(1911–1991)

Donald Paul Haden
cycle and motor vehicle
parts manufacturer
(b. 1941)

Peter Haden
hotelier in Ireland
(b. 1941)

John Haden
(adopted son)
domestic appliance manufacturer
(1943–2013)

Simon-Peter Haden
hotelier in Ireland
(b. 1966)

CHAPTER ONE
Early Days: Making and Racing Bicycles

And did the Countenance Divine, shine forth upon our clouded hills?
And was Jerusalem builded here, among these dark Satanic Mills?

(William Blake, 1804)

It was on 23 April 1851 that George Haden was born in the small industrial town of Wordsley, Staffordshire, the son of William Haden and his wife Sarah. The family were very typical of their generation, working in the local glass industry, but with close connections with friends and relations who worked on the west side of Birmingham where similar skills were employed. William had himself been born in Birmingham in 1821 and baptised in St Philip's Cathedral, not far from Hockley where the Birmingham glass industry was concentrated at that time.

George was one of seven children born to William and Sarah and he followed his father into the glass industry where he was employed initially as a 'stopperer' making tops for wine decanters before graduating to the more skilled occupation of glass cutter. His father, William, was a master glass cutter and a partner in the glass cutting firm Parrish Lowe and Haden based in Wordsley.

As a young man, George would have been aware of the new phenomenon of velocipede racing that swept the nation in the 1860s, and which was becoming such a major sport in Wolverhampton and the surrounding areas where special race

St Philips Cathedral, Birmingham.

tracks were built and supported by local firms who were involved in the manufacturing and development of these new machines.

The racing of high wheel bicycles (later to be known as penny-farthings or ordinaries) had become a spectacular sport enjoyed by large crowds. Usually run on quarter-mile cinder tracks, one-, two- and three-mile races were held with riders often being handicapped according to earlier performance. Occasionally, ten-mile races were held and competition was so keen that it was not unknown for riders to be doped, or for bicycles to be interfered with—tightening the small back wheel being a favourite ploy.

Race meetings were held throughout the country, but the Molineaux

Grounds in Wolverhampton became one of the most important venues, attracting the best amateurs and professionals. Another well-established Midlands track was Aston Lower Grounds in Birmingham, which became a well-known course used for championship races. We can only guess that these might have both been popular destinations for George Haden and his friends to watch—and possibly take part in—races.

It has long been said within the Haden family that George started making bicycles in 1869 and this is supported by company sales literature published in 1921 stating that the business had been in existence for 'over fifty years'. An old nameplate  mounted on the wall outside the Princip Street factory, photographed in the 1920s, confirms that bicycles had indeed been manufactured since 1869, and also that the Haden brand name 'New Comet' had been used on bicycles before being applied to Haden motorcycles.

In 1869, George was living in Chapel Street, Wordsley, moving to the Hockley area of Birmingham in 1873 having married local girl Sarah Heeley. There are, however, no records to indicate precisely what he produced, and it was not until the publication of the 1882 Birmingham Kelly's Trade Directory that he was first recorded as a bicycle maker, living at Barr Street West in the Hockley district of Birmingham, having previously continued to be listed as a glass cutter. In accordance with the custom at that time, it is likely that he operated from a small workshop inside the house or attached at the rear. It was quite common in those days for a man to have more than one job, and most likely would give as his occupation that which at any particular period accounted for the larger part of his hours or income.

In 1886 George moved to Smith Street renting a workshop nearby, and by 1897 was describing himself additionally as a manufacturer of tricycles. In about 1891 he moved to larger premises in nearby Harford Street and went into partnership with Frank Podmore as bicycle makers.

The family's keen interest in cycling is well-illustrated by the inclusion of George together with his two sons William and Alfred in a photograph taken in 1895 of the members of The Princes End and District Cycling Club which had been founded in 1892. The club was

The Princes End and District Cycling Club. Season 1895.

based in Princes End, a coal mining area in the Black Country, about two miles north of Dudley.

In the early days Wolverhampton, Coventry and Birmingham were all important centres for the manufacture of bicycles and component parts. By 1894 the *London Times* was reporting that 'cycle manufacture has now attained large proportion in Birmingham, which has supplanted Coventry as the chief seat of the trade. While production increases from year to year, profits are steadily declining.'

Entry into the bicycle trade was relatively simple and the steady growth in demand attracted many businesses and entrepreneurs. It was said that 'the average mechanic with an attic and a length or two of gas pipe could soon become a full-blown cycle maker,' and a map of Birmingham, dated 1897, in the possession of the author illustrates the location and names of 190 businesses said to be involved in the cycle trade.

In the course of researching for this book, several early family connections with the cycle industry have been discovered. For instance, a great uncle of the author named Thomas Lawley was a bicycle chain manufacturer in the Jewellery Quarter in Birmingham around the turn of the century, later specialising in the production of medals and other parts from nickel silver.

Although 1896 was regarded as a boom year for cycle companies, an entry in the *London Gazette* of 19 June that year records:

> . . . the partnership heretofore subsisting between . . . George Joseph Haden and Frank Laurence Podmore carrying on business as Cycle Manufacturers at Comet Works 39 Harford-street Birmingham under the style or firm of Haden and Podmore has been dissolved by mutual consent . . . and all debts . . . will be paid by the said Frank Laurence Podmore.

Despite this business break up, the families remained close and in 1951 Sidney, grandson of George, married Cicely Podmore.

Following the split from Podmores in 1896, George decided to retire and two of his sons William and Alfred, determined to continue the business, set themselves up as bicycle manufacturers in new premises at 54 Staniforth Street, later moving to 49 Princip Street. Times were, however, becoming difficult due to an over supply to the market, made worse by an influx of cheap American imports. An entry in the *London Gazette* dated 14 November 1899 records:

> NOTICE is hereby given, that the Partnership heretofore existing between us the undersigned, Alfred Hamlet Haden and William George Haden, in the trade or business of Cycle Manufacturers, carried on by us at The New Comet Cycle Works, 49, Princip-street, in the city of Birmingham, under the firm of Haden Brothers, was dissolved on the 30th day of June last. All debts due and owing by the late firm will be received and paid by the undersigned Alfred Hamlet Haden by whom the business will in future be carried on at the New Comet Cycle Works aforesaid under the style of A. H. Haden.

It seems quite probable that their father, George, still had some interest in the business, and we know that by this time they were concerned not just with the manufacture of complete bicycles, but also of cycle accessories. Unfortunately, George was suffering from ill health and died in a nursing home in Sutton Coldfield on 21 August 1903, aged only fifty-two. Two years later, his eldest son, William, set sail from Liverpool to Montreal on the steamship *Bavaria,* emigrating to Canada to start a new life. He and his wife, Hattie, later had a son who worked in California for the Columbia Cycle Company.

This left the enthusiastic Alfred free to develop the business in his own way. He had already started to work on the idea of fitting a small internal combustion engine into a bicycle frame, but it soon became evident that a stronger frame was required, which he made using larger diameter tubes. These required larger fittings to join the tubular parts together, and although it is not known when the family first made cycle frame components, there is evidence to suggest that by 1900 these had become a Haden speciality. They were soon to become the mainstay of the business, running alongside the production of bicycles, motorcycles and other products.

Agnes Haden,
daughter of James Speed.

But tragedy was to follow. Alfred lost his first wife, Annie, in 1903 shortly after she gave birth to their second son, Sidney. He was, however, fortunate to soon meet a very capable new partner, Agnes Speed. She was the daughter of James Speed, a local glassworks manager, who had earlier spent some years in the Far East teaching the Japanese how to make glass, a craft already well-known to the Haden family.

CHAPTER TWO
The Glass Years: Haden Family Involvement in the Glass Industry at Home and Abroad
by Sally Haden

Although the pivotal years of the Haden family's transition from glass into cycles have been described in chapter one, it will be valuable to pause at this point and look a little more deeply into the glass industry of the time. This chapter describes the family's relationship to the Victorian glass industry not only in Britain, but also in far-off Japan. Section one of this chapter sheds more light on George Haden's ancestors in glass, while section two discusses the interesting life of a Scottish glassmaker who married into the family.

Since at least the opening of the nineteenth century, the Hadens had been closely involved with glassmaking in the Stourbridge area to the west of Birmingham, where they were glass cutters. Their home was Wordsley, one of a string of small towns that stretches for about seven miles from the town of Stourbridge in the south up to Dudley in the north, each community being deeply committed to glass at that time. The district as a whole was, and still is, described as the Stourbridge Glass District. It is set in the larger industrial area called the Black Country, which covers parts of South Staffordshire and Worcestershire, on the west side of Birmingham.

The area is commonly held to be the heart of the Industrial Revolution. After witnessing its thousands of smoking chimneys, dark spoil heaps, open sewers and fiery red foundries and forges in the 1860s, Elihu Burritt, the American Consul to Birmingham, said it was 'black by day and red by night'—thus it became known as the Black Country. Its riches of coal, iron, clay, sand and lime gave birth to an outpouring of everything that could be made of metal. A river of nails, chains, tools, steel, and machines turned the wider region into the 'workshop of the world'.

It was to the Black Country that a Scottish glassmaker named James Speed moved with his family, just around the time when George Haden first set himself up in Birmingham in the 1870s. Some thirty years later the two families were to be joined by the marriage of James's daughter Agnes to George's son, Alfred. The couple probably met on the streets of Aston, a brand new suburb to the north of Birmingham's centre, to which both families moved as the century drew to a close. The children of the union were Mildred (1906–1996), Victor (1909–1972) and twins Denis and Donald (1911–1991), Donald being the father of the author.

George was still alive when Alfred married Agnes in 1903, and so must have met his son's new father-in-law. Because of his own background in glass, George would have been fascinated to hear James speak about the years when he went to the other side of the world to teach glassmaking in an alien land. How enthralled they must have been to know why and how all that happened. For although in the early years of the twentieth century James Speed was the manager of an Aston glassworks, from 1879 to 1883 he worked in Japan with a much greater responsibility. He played a leading role in the development of that country's first western-style glass factory, advising, assisting and instructing Japanese glassmakers at the request of their newly-established, modernising government.

Section One
Three Generations of Glass Cutters
and the Haden Family's First Known Business

'You see, Tom . . . the world goes on at a smarter pace now than
it did when I was a young fellow . . . It's this steam you see.'
(Mr Deane in George Eliot's *The Mill on the Floss*)

Wordsley

At the time of George Haden's birth in the late spring of 1851, the
district into which he was born was one of the most important glass
manufacturing areas in Britain. Few places in the country could compete
with Stourbridge glass for its combination of quality and quantity. The
family home in Wordsley was surrounded by several huge brick cones
where the finest quality crystal glassware was made. In the 1850s Wordsley
itself had so many glass cutters that it might be said to have been the
capital of glass cutting in the West Midlands.

Stourbridge was rich in glassmaking history. This was where Protestant
Huguenot glassmakers settled after they fled the religious wars of Europe
at the end of the sixteenth century. They had been attracted to its ideal
combination of the resources that were necessary for glassmaking: high
quality refractory clay, coal, sand and limestone. By the 1850s, a number

View of Wordsley in about 1900, looking south or southeast. The large brick cones belonged to
the various glass factories. (Courtesy of Broadfield House Glass Museum, Dudley MBC.)

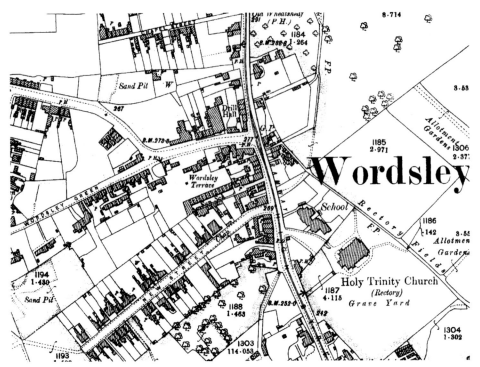

Old map of the upper part of Wordsley. The Haden family were living in Wordsley Green in 1841 and in Chapel Street (at the top of the map) after that. The Parrish, Lowe & Haden cutting business was in New Street.

of companies had already been thriving for over a hundred years and were exporting their products across the globe. Generations of glassmakers and cutters in the area had grown up in an environment of full employment.

In fact, the Haden family's link to Stourbridge glass probably stretches back into the eighteenth century. Although details are sketchy until the 1841 census, that survey makes it clear that George's father and grandfather were well-established as glass cutters in Wordsley, apparently having been born locally.

Richard Haden (1798–1843) and the Application of Steam to Cutting

The first Haden ancestor known for certain to have worked in the glass industry was George's grandfather Richard Haden. He would have been a boy of about eight when he had his first working day amongst the glass cutters, perhaps being put to operate the handle which turned the worker's wheel. Until thirty or forty years into the nineteenth century, the machinery was mostly operated by hand or foot, and workshops were predominantly either inside cutters' houses or in their backyards. Thinly blown glassware (known as 'blanks') which were supplied by or bought from the manufacturers, were 'cut' or decorated very delicately in low relief. It took years to master the skills, and such finely-wrought objects were expensive to buy.

But major changes were on the way, thanks to the widespread application of steam power to industry during the Industrial Revolution. In 1789, shortly before Richard's birth, an engine powered by steam was used to drive a glass cutting lathe for the first time in Britain, in a Dudley factory. Now boosted by greater energy, cutting could go deep into thick lead glass, creating very effective simple or elaborate patterns with relative ease. For the tables of the rich, huge suites of expensive, sparkling and weighty lead glass could now be made in the time that it used to take to produce just a small handful of items. Manufacturers began to establish in-house cutting from about 1820, a more industrial form of production where everything could be kept under close control within the factory.

The fashion was set for this fine product, signalling a boom in the glass industry. Regency glass—as it became known—was very popular amongst the wealthy and made English glass famous around the world. Additionally, a wide range of reasonably priced ware came on the market for the burgeoning middle classes.

This new factory model for fine glassmaking was popular amongst manufacturers in Birmingham, who quickly set up in-house cutting workshops. Richard migrated with his family to the town in about 1821, maybe in order to take advantage of the opportunity. But then he returned home for good in about 1829, perhaps because the large glass company Richardsons of Wordsley, which had an in-house cutting shop, was thriving and he could get steady work there.

William Hamlet Haden (1821–1866) and the Family's First Known Business

Richard's second son, William Hamlet Haden, was born during the family's sojourn in Birmingham. By the middle of the century, William was a family man with several children and had worked in Wordsley's glass cutting trade since he was a teenager. With fine glass selling well nationally and with a family to support, he was probably considering a new option which was already being tried out in the district—if he was not already involved in it.

For the ways of the industry were changing rapidly. Cutting by steam power had introduced a much more industrial feel to glassmaking and glass cutters saw that they could set themselves up in business, independent of the big companies. Instead of working on their own from home, they could lease a small cutting shop that was completely separate from the factories and establish a modest business that stood between the individual craftsman and the big businesses. These middle men were a new breed of glass workers.

Robert Ball ARCA, RE, RBA, RBSA, RWA, *Glass Cutting, Stuart's Crystal, Stourbridge*, 1937, etching. This cutting shop design was developed early in the nineteenth century and remained in use until the early 1950s. It would have been very familiar to the Hadens. (With thanks to the artist's daughter Ros Smith, and Broadfield House Glass Museum, Dudley MBC.)

Since the 1789 introduction of steam power to cutting, Birmingham engineers Boulton & Watt had been working to reduce the size and cost of the early engines to make them affordable for smaller glassworks. Although these engines were too expensive for the home worker, a middle man with partners could afford the models that were coming out by the 1850s, or at least he could afford to lease a premises which had one.

A compact engine set in its own boiler house outside the workshop would drive a shaft running down the centre of the workshop inside. This in turn would power the cutters' lathes set out in two rows, one on either

Left, modern glasscutting workshops are light, well ventilated and equipped with safe machinery. (With thanks to Kevin Barry Adams, Ruskin Glass Centre, Stourbridge.)

Right, pair of antique silver-topped glass decanters in a modern glass restoration workshop at Ruskin Mill Glass Centre, Stourbridge. Having lost their original stoppers, they await the attention of the restorer who, like George Haden, has the job of cutting and grinding blank stoppers and grinding the necks of the decanters, to make the one fit the other perfectly.

side, by means of rotating belts. The proprietor purchased blanks from glassmakers, had them decorated by his employees and sold them onward, either direct to salesmen or shops, or to a big manufacturer with whom he might have a contract.

But any cutter who set himself up in such a business was in danger of ruffling feathers in the community. By moving up in the world in this way, becoming an entrepreneur and an employer, he was stepping out of line with his neighbours. Cutters' families with whom he had grown up, or even married into, might become his employees. Suddenly, he was a master, a man in control of his own fate, and therefore dangerously set against the old, small ways.

William Haden must have been a man of courage and foresight, unafraid to step up the class ladder, even to embroil his family in local disputes. On 14 May 1859, together with two other glass men, he signed a lease for an independent cutting premises in the centre of Wordsley and

TO

ALL WHOM IT MAY CONCERN.

Several parties in Brettell Lane and Wordsley having advertized for a number of Boys, from 14 to 16 years of age, under the pretence of learning them the Art of **FLINT GLASS CUTTING**: we,

THE

GLASS CUTTERS

feel it to be our duty to inform the Public that our Members left those Shops, being satisfied that the system under which they were working was detrimental to the interests of the Trade at large, and calculated finally to produce most ruinous consequences; our Members only desired to Work by the Piece, which the Employers thought proper to refuse, thereby causing the present dissatisfaction. The Employers alluded to are termed *Middle Men*, or *Small Masters*, standing between the Manufacturer and the Workman in our Trade, more especially in some of the Shops connected with the Manufactories of this District; the men have suffered most severely from this state of things, and we consider it to be our bounden duty to put an end to such a ruinous system, and we trust that the Working Men of other Trades will not aid or assist in any way to encourage any system that is injurious to the Rights of Labour.

BY ORDER OF THE COMMITTEE

OF THE UNITED FLINT GLASS CUTTERS' SOCIETY,

July 2nd, 1857.   WORDSLEY BRANCH.

THOMAS MELLARD, PRINTER, STOURBRIDGE.

Glass cutters' union poster, 1857.

thus the first known Haden family business was born. A full transcription of the lease can be found in the appendix of this book.

William and his partners made this choice even though only two years earlier a bitter argument had erupted in Wordsley about the very sort of business which William was now establishing. A poster published at the time shows that members of the local branch of the United Flint Glass Cutters' Society walked out of their factory jobs, protesting at the attempt by 'Middle Men or Small Masters' to employ 'a number of Boys, from 14 to 16 years of age, under the pretence of learning them the art of Flint Glass Cutting'. William was now one of the hated 'middle men or small masters.'

The lease which established William Haden firmly in business in 1859 was for a property in New Street, only a few minutes walk from Chapel Street where the family was living around that time. His partners were James Parrish, the son of a master glass cutter of Bristol, and William Lowe, a glass cutter and close neighbour of the Hadens. The premises were already established as an independent cutting workshop with all the appropriate equipment, including an eight-horse-power engine, but it was apparently about to be extended, perhaps to accommodate as many as twenty-five or thirty workers. A directory of 1865 lists the business as 'Parrish, Lowe & Haden, glass cutters, Wordsley.'

Parrish was the principle of the business, for censuses say he was employing ten men and three boys in 1861; and thirteen men, fourteen boys, and one woman half-time in 1871. From this it seems that the company prospered and the partners' confidence had been justified. The cutters' strikes of the period ended in defeat for the workers.

Industrial Unrest and William Haden's Achievement

William's success must be set against the wider picture. The changing manufacturing techniques which had come in with the Industrial Revolution in many types of industry across the country had brought with them great challenges to the ways of the craftsmen. Workers found themselves under threat in many respects. Their time-honoured and carefully guarded methods were being upset by factory owners—and few industries had craftsmen more rooted in strict and ancient traditions than glassmaking. Stourbridge had the greatest concentration of the best skilled

Left, George Haden's grave, Witton Cemetery, Birmingham. He died on 21 August 1903.

Right, a flint glass jug in the family's possession thought to have been engraved by George Haden circa 1870.

glass men in Britain, men whose working practices had changed little since they were evolved in the forests of Bohemia centuries earlier. At the same time, the district had a number of glass manufacturers or masters who were profiting from the boom times and looking to modernise. A clash was inevitable.

When William had his business in the early 1860s, labour unrest was widespread in Britain's glass industry. In Stourbridge it involved glassmakers and cutters alike, as their societies or unions began to object in particular to the increasing numbers of apprentices taken on by the big glass masters. These were more than could be trained properly. A very serious disagreement which started in Stourbridge in 1858 and spread across Britain for almost a year, involved the lock out of thousands of glassmakers and (by default, because there was no glass to decorate) glass cutters. A dispute of the previous year that had only involved glass cutters would certainly have affected the Haden family. Moreover, this trouble was slow to abate. A much worse strike lasting for nearly a year broke out in Dudley in 1865, after two cutters who were active in their union left their in-house factory job in order to set up a cutting 'sweatshop', and immediately broke the union's rules on apprentices.

Against the backdrop of such trouble, it is all the more remarkable that William Haden stepped out to form a business—one that may have been the first in the family. Early business records are very hard to find in archives, and maybe Richard Haden or an earlier ancestor took the first step. But nevertheless, the cutting shop of Parish, Lowe & Haden on New Street, Wordsley, must surely have impressed George Haden, his second son. It would have given George the courage to lead the family forward just as his father had done, if in an entirely new direction—into bicycles.

Death, Disease and Moving On

Death played a marked hand in the family story in 1866. After just seven years in Parrish, Lowe & Haden, and at the age of only forty-four, William passed away from disease. But such early deaths were common amongst glass cutters. The work was not healthy and the cutting shop was a dangerous place: not only could the revolving power belts easily trap a worker's arm causing very serious injury but, more insidiously, the air was poisonous. It contained lead from the special powder used in the final polishing process. A letter from the Flint Glass Cutter's Union in Wordsley dated 1872, asking the manufacturers for shorter working hours because of the poor conditions, paints a graphic picture:

> You, Gentlemen, are fully cognizant of the fact of the unhealthiness of our Trade; we are constantly, or nearly so, in sitting posture, breathing vitiated air, causing in consequence—Dropped Hands, Cholic, and almost innumerable diseases . . . Terrible, Gentlemen, is it not? to suffer from diseases which for ever prevent us from supporting our Wives and Little-ones; many of us at all ages, are forced to leave the Trade through its unhealthiness . . .

It was not until much later in the century that manufacturers began to install ventilation, too late for almost all of the Haden cutters. William's father Richard had died at a similar age, and his son George was to die at fifty-two. The only Hadens born in the Victorian period who lived to a good age were the women, and those men who were not cutters.

William's 'little-ones' that he left behind ranged in age from twenty-one down to only three. One was a glass cutter who died only two years later, just nineteen when they buried him. The sudden loss of her husband and son—seeing so starkly how the trade could cut a worker down like that—must have given William's wife Sarah much worry about the future for her remaining children. But change was afoot for all of them.

Her eldest daughter Hannah had just married into a family by the name of Quarry which had deep roots in Birmingham, but which, like so many other cutting families, frequently migrated between the town and Wordsley. By the early 1870s both Hannah and George Haden were sampling urban life in Birmingham, thanks to the support of those members of the Quarry family who were already settled and prosperous there. By moving to the town, these siblings were following in their grandfather's footsteps, though unlike his grandfather, George never returned to Wordsley to live.

Perhaps Sarah encouraged all her children to seek better places and occupations, for during the 1870s and 1880s one son left for America, another joined George in Birmingham for a while in order to learn jewellery-making, and she took the two youngest up north, to where iron and steel making was booming.

George himself, as we know from earlier in this book, had already made a strong commitment to bicycle-making. Nevertheless, the censuses tell us that in 1871 he was working as a 'stopperer at glassworks', still living at home in Wordsley. He was nineteen then, so had been breathing in the lead-poisoned air of the cutting shop every workday for a few years already, and was to continue to do so for several more, until finally his hard work with bicycles in Birmingham paid off. His cycle-making business was strong enough in the 1880s for him to stop cutting, but it seems the damage was already done. George Haden died at only fifty-two years-of-age, of kidney problems probably brought on by his work in glass, leaving his son Alfred to take over the bicycle business.

Section Two
James Speed and the Japanese Connection

'He went to Japan to larn 'em.'

James Speed, whose daughter would marry bicycle maker Alfred Haden in 1903, was a Scottish Presbyterian, a glassmaker by trade and a confident man. In the Haden family it was said of him that 'he went to Japan to larn 'em' and investigations have confirmed that for four years he was involved in an extraordinary project first set up in Tokyo in 1873. He was one of four British glass experts who were appointed to help, advise and instruct at the Shinagawa Glass Works, Japan's very first fully western-style, industrial glass plant, an enterprise which was to revolutionise Japanese glassmaking.

Such a task would require courage, patience and skill. To travel all the way to the Far East, to attempt to train men who could not speak English, to help set up a factory which was extremely innovative for Japan at the time—these were just some of the difficulties he would have had to encounter. Simply living there was a challenge, because until the 1850s Japan had been closed to the rest of the world for centuries and it was quite a dangerous place for westerners. When the country was prized opened by the Americans who wished to trade, quickly followed in by the British and the other European powers, many Japanese people wanted to forcibly repel the 'hairy barbarians', as westerners were known. The samurai sword might be waiting for any westerner down a dark street.

It would be natural to imagine that a person capable of this kind of responsibility would come from a reasonably fortunate background with a stable home and some education. Or at least he would have had a father already established in glassmaking, able to lead the way. Research into James's early life, however, reveals none of these advantages. Born approximately ten miles to the west of Glasgow in about 1834, his childhood was marred by significant poverty. Furthermore, it is probable that he was illegitimate. According to information reliably passed down in the family, he was 'born on the wrong side of the blanket' to the Buccleuch family, Scottish nobles related to the British Royal Family. His birth certificate

Left, this portrait of James Speed was retained by one of his Japanese apprentices, Magoichi Shimada, out of respect for his teacher. Shimada's son wrote on it 'Meiji 12–16 (1879–83), Shinagawa Glassworks, Mr James Speed, British, my father's teacher.' (With thanks to Osamu Shimada.)

Right, the Speed family lived in west Glasgow when James was a child. The building on the left is the actual tenement building on the corner of Kelvingrove Street and Argyle Street. A tenement consisted of several flats, often with large families crammed into each flat.

has never been found. His mother and sisters were frequently destitute and ill; one of James's sisters was even in jail for a while. The man listed in the 1841 census as his father, David Speed, went from job to job taking whatever manual work he could find. James's childhood home in Glasgow in the 1840s was an inauspicious start to life.

Starting Out in Glass

It is unclear how James got into glassmaking. It was difficult for a boy to begin in the glasshouse without having either a relative in the trade or sponsorship. But start he did and he must have been good at it, because at least by 1859 he was a glassmaker journeyman in Edinburgh, resident amongst some of Scotland's most highly skilled flint glass craftsmen. Further, by 1866 he was at the West Lothian Flint Glass Works in Bathgate where fine quality lead-crystal glassware was made and where he became works manager. Thirteen years later he took a ship to Japan to assist in the development of that country's first western-style industrial glassworks.

Such a rise was not particularly uncommon in those days, Victorian times being characterised by daring, inventiveness, self-reliance, and hard work. A man could easily improve his lot through the determined application of his will-power, and acquire a good education, money and respect, even if he had not been born to those assets. Undoubtedly, James must have been naturally talented as a craftsman, but one circumstance in his life gives a possible clue to his strong advance. His marriage certificate shows that he had a link to the Freemasons.

In August 1859, when James married Mary Ross, the daughter of an Edinburgh stonemason, the ceremony was held in the Grand Lodge of the Scottish Freemasons on George Street, Edinburgh. This was also the home of Mary and her widowed mother at that date. It is possible that Mary and her mother had been offered the small flat at the back of the Lodge upon the death of her father, a mason by trade and probably a Freemason. It may be that James was encouraged to become a Freemason when the couple met. The other possibility is that he was sponsored by the Freemasons when he was young—perhaps after David Speed's death—and may have been educated or given an apprenticeship in glass as part of this charitable patronage. Alternatively, his biological father—said to be a Buccleuch—perhaps had a hand in his advance, either through the Freemasons or otherwise.

Although it has not been possible to prove any of this, and James's early years remain largely a mystery, even the limited contact he had with the Grand Lodge through his wife would have been useful, to give him confidence and probably some valuable contacts. Again, it is not known precisely how he heard about the job in Japan or how he was recruited, whether through his Bathgate work or through other contacts, but evidence suggests that it was during 1872, while he was still at Bathgate, that James first learned of the plan for a glass factory in Japan.

Why Did the Japanese Want Western Glassmaking?

At that time the Japanese were making major enquiries in the West about numerous types of technology which they desired to have in their own country. They wanted to bridge the chasm between themselves and the rest of the world which had developed during more than two centuries of self-imposed isolation from all other lands, a time when Japanese industry had become restricted to local, craft-based work, making mainly high-status items by hand. In the case of glass, for example, Japan knew almost nothing about window glass making because, since early times, paper screens had been used instead of windows. Made of paper and bamboo, these *shoji* screens let in the light and could slide on runners, but they were opaque and stretched from floor to ceiling like walls. Before westernisation, very rich people had tiny windows carefully inserted into their *shojis,* but they were entirely decorative and precious, made using small pieces of imported glass. And thanks to centuries of using pottery and wood for home utensils, domestic glassware of any sort was very largely unknown.

The rapid transfer of western knowledge to a technologically backward country, such as Japan, was, of course, fraught with problems. The Industrial Revolution in the West had taken a very long time to evolve and depended on the incremental growth of many elements, such as local networks, economic and transport infrastructure, countless inventions, and the opening up of global trade. The abrupt introduction into Japan of industries such as cotton spinning, iron and steel mills, steam engines, railways, and shipbuilding was very difficult, but the Japanese were extremely determined—both to import the technology which would make Japan self-sufficient, and to pull their nation out of a feudal economy. But they also wanted to own that technology itself, and be in control of their own growth process. They were very aware of the negative effects on China that had resulted from the recent Opium Wars, when western powers had brought Japan's great neighbour to its knees and opened it up to rapacious trade.

So when a group of top Japanese government ministers visited Britain in 1872 to investigate how their country could modernise, seeking information from not only the British government, but also from dozens of factories and various sorts of institutions, they did not invite large companies to invest in Japan. Instead, they sought individual experts, men who were happy to be employed on short contracts—commonly two years—and then return home again. The experts' job was to instruct, assist and advise in Japanese-owned enterprises. Therefore, while the ministers in 1872 spent a great deal of time at, for instance, Chance Brothers' leading glassworks near Birmingham, none of the four men who actually went to instruct and advise on glassmaking in Japan were from big glass companies.

The Glassworks at Shinagawa

The glassworks at which James Speed was to supervise from 1879 to 1883 was in the fishing village of Shinagawa, now a district of Tokyo. The site was beside Japan's first railway line which had opened in 1872, a short track running north from the port of Yokohama to Tokyo. Two Japanese businessmen had set up the factory in 1873, intending to profit from the manufacture of their country's first window glass, a commodity much needed once modernisation had begun. Using British trading company Jardine Matheson as their agent, they applied to England for help in planning the factory, purchasing and shipping materials, and engaging glassmakers.

Shinagawa Glassworks photographed in about 1881, beside Japan's first railway line opened in 1872. (Reprinted by courtesy of Ozawa Takeshi.)

The first British glassmaker to arrive was a Manchester manufacturer named Thomas Walton, whose family had been in the glass industry for at least a century. His main tasks during his time at Shinagawa from 1874 to 1878 were establishing the furnaces and attempting to make the first window glass. Unfortunately, success with the glass proved extremely elusive. Although the Japanese trainees were already experienced in glass blowing, they did not have the special skill and strength which it took to manipulate the large amount of glass necessary to make a sheet—a skill which took years to acquire. In fact, despite repeated very costly trials, it was not until early in the twentieth century that Japan was able to make its first sheet glass for windows.

In 1876 the Shinagawa glassworks was nationalised and its goals

SS *Royal Charter*, a ship very similar to the SS *Hong Kong* in which Mrs Walton and her five young children travelled to join her husband, Thomas Walton, in Japan. On entering the Indian Ocean, the Hong Kong hit a rock and foundered very rapidly at dawn on 22 February 1875, Mrs Walton and the children being sucked into the depths with the undertow. (Image with thanks to Wales Online.)

redefined. In addition to sheet glass trials, the factory was to start developing flint glass: at first red signal glass for ships' lights and then, later, all kinds of domestic and utilitarian ware. A great emphasis was put on the training of Japanese glassmakers so that they could subsequently go on to establish themselves as glassmakers and manufacturers across Japan. A crucible-maker from Stourbridge named Elijah Skidmore arrived to assist and instruct, and Thomas Walton was replaced by James Speed in 1879. The last expert of the four was Emanuel Hauptmann, a highly skilled Bohemian engraver and cutter who gave instruction between 1881 and 1882.

Unfortunately, research has not yet revealed precisely how any of these men were found and why they were chosen, but it is clear that James and Thomas knew each other well. In 1871 while James was working at Bathgate, Thomas Walton's brother was his manager and it may have been shortly after this that they heard about the Japan project. By early 1873, James had taken his family south to live in Dudley close to the factory of Britain's leading window glass manufacturer at that time, Chance Brothers. Although he could have moved to Dudley to work for any of the lead-crystal glassworks in the Stourbridge glass district, it is possible that he was there in order to develop his knowledge of window glass making at Chance Brothers. Then, once the Shinagawa glassworks was up and running, he could more effectively provide training to the Japanese.

Another possibility is that James's departure for Shinagawa was postponed in an effort to reduce costs. The establishment of a sheet glassmaking factory was not cheap anywhere, but in Japan it was extremely expensive, and proved to be more so as the project progressed. So perhaps it was decided to stagger the arrival of the experts, and hope that it could be kick-started with just Thomas and the crucible-maker. Whatever the reasons, James spent nearly seven years in Dudley before setting sail for the Far East in 1879.

Although the opening of the Suez Canal ten years earlier had made the journey considerably less arduous, bringing it down to about six weeks, such voyages could still be dangerous. Thomas Walton's wife and his five children—who were aged from thirteen down to only four years old—had been lost at sea when their ship sank *en route* to join him in Japan, so with this precedent it is not surprising that James's wife and children stayed behind in the Black Country. Unless James returned for an unrecorded short visit, he did not see them again for over four years. Upon his departure, his youngest child Agnes—the future wife of Alfred Haden—was just a toddler. Upon his return she was seven years old.

A Sophisticated Glassmaker

James Speed was highly thought of in Japan. Shortly after his arrival at Shinagawa, a local newspaper reported that he was 'more sophisticated in terms of manufacturing technique than his predecessor [Thomas Walton],' and to this day the family of one of his trainees preserves a portrait of him out of respect for his work. With the assistance of the crucible-maker and the Bohemian engraver, James trained dozens of Japanese glassmakers in western techniques. Pressing, moulding, cutting and engraving equipment was imported, along with various oxides to introduce new colours. In 1881 the factory exhibited nearly three hundred items at a national trade fair: tableware, lamps, lanterns, bottles, vases, glass for pharmaceutical use or chemical experiments, ships' sidelights, and stationary objects.

But sheet glass, the one product which could have made the factory truly viable, failed again and again, causing the government to shut

Two brush holders known to have been made at the Shinagawa glassworks during the period of James Speed's instruction. Lead glass. Heights: 168mm and 148mm. (With thanks to Tokyo National Museum.)

Photograph taken in 1883 of glassmakers at the Shinagawa Glass Works, Tokyo. Sitting at centre left is James Speed, their British instructor. (Reprinted by courtesy of Meijimura Museum.)

the facility and put it up for sale in 1883. Elijah Skidmore had already moved to Osaka at the invitation of a Japanese glass manufacturer named Keishin Ito who was setting up a similar factory. James followed, together with several of his trainees, and gave instruction there to about thirty Japanese glassmakers. This factory developed along such similar lines to Shinagawa that it became popularly known as 'Little Shinagawa'. One of James's trainees who had followed him to Osaka, Magoichi Shimada, bought the business in about 1887 and established what became a top Japanese glass manufacturing company in the twentieth century. It was owned by the Shimada family through three generations, and the modern company Toyo Glass Co. Ltd. can trace its history through the Shimadas right back to James Speed. Today the Osaka region is where most of Japan's glass is made.

The Shinagawa factory itself was purchased by a Japanese investor named Katsuzo Nishimura in 1884. He was successful for a few years with bottle-making and a wide range of tableware, but had to sell it off in 1892 following a national economic crash. Other Japanese glassmakers, each of whom had links with Shinagawa, experimented long and hard with sheet glass, finally finding success for their country in about 1909.

Back Home

Japan's policy of national self-determination did not permit foreign experts to stay beyond their limited contracts, so Elijah and James soon returned home from Osaka, at least before 1885. James's family may have still been in Dudley then, but by 1891, when the next national census was taken, they had moved into Aston just north of the centre of Birmingham. The brand-new terraced house at 66 Aston Brook Street had the latest conveniences, together with three bedrooms, a living room, a parlour, and a kitchen. Moreover, it was situated where it was easy for the growing family to get work. James himself was away in Edinburgh at that date, where his census address suggests he was working for the prestigious company Royal Holyrood Glass Works.

The census that was taken ten years later on 31 March 1901 paints a different picture of the Speed family. James was at home with his wife and children, but they were now living in the next street, an even newer road of good quality terraced houses. There, at 127 Bracebridge Street, the census enumerator found James to be employed as a glassworks manager. He was age sixty-six, and amongst his offspring, his youngest daughter, Agnes, was a twenty-three-year-old tailoress.

Back in Aston Brook Street, at number 107, the enumerator on that same day in 1901 met a young couple—bicycle maker Alfred Haden and his wife, Annie. In a sudden stroke of fate, tragedy was to unite the two households: Annie died shortly after giving birth to her second child in November that year. A young man with two infant children could not be left without a wife for long and Alfred was a good catch, a bicycle manufacturer with prospects. A match was soon made, and in January 1903 James Speed led his daughter Agnes to the altar, giving her away in marriage to the Haden family.

Family memories and photographs of Agnes Speed suggest that she was a spirited and determined woman. It is believed she gave Alfred strength, both in his business and in providing him with four more children, one of whom was Donald William Haden, father of

Left, Tokyo glass blowers working beside the furnace in one of the very few such glassworks in Japan today (2015), making fine tableware. Production methods are almost identical to those first introduced by the British at the Shinagawa factory in the late nineteenth century. (With thanks to Tajima Glass Co. Ltd.)

Right, Memorial on the site of the Shinagawa glassworks, Tokyo. (With thanks to Michael Stevens.)

the author. Her firm character may be accounted for in part by her Scottish and Presbyterian background, but she must have been much influenced by her father and his exceptional achievements.

Today, Shinagawa is one of Tokyo's many suburbs. Beside the railway line which carried Japan's first train in 1872, and tucked in next to a large white modern building, stands a memorial to the glassworks which James Speed helped to establish. Set up by Sankyo Pharmaceutical Company, the present owner of the glassworks site, it commemorates the significant efforts which were made there in the late Victorian period to kick-start the country's glass industry. For any passer-by, the engraved stones of the monument speak quietly of the remarkable time when Japan first began to make modern glass with the help of four British glassmakers.

James Speed was buried in 1908 at Witton Cemetery, Aston, Birmingham.

Japanese glassblowers working beside the furnace. Date unknown but probably representative of flint glassmaking at Shinagawa under James Speed. (Reprinted with thanks to Meijimura Museum.)

CHAPTER THREE
The Motorcycle Years: Designing and Manufacturing Motorcycles and Sidecars, 1903–1931

Our standard model AI is now practically copied
by every motorcycle manufacturing firm of repute.

(Alfred Haden in his 1914 sales brochure)

It was in 1903 that, following the tragic loss of his first wife, Annie, Alfred Haden married the daughter of glassmaker James Speed. His new domestic arrangements left him free to concentrate on developing his business; the early success of which is indicated by his move to larger premises in Princip Street in the Birmingham gun manufacturing quarter.

By this time, Birmingham had the largest number of bicycle and component manufacturers in Britain. The larger cycle manufacturers made many of their own components on site, while the smaller builders relied on buying in parts from the new cycle component industry, which had developed as a result of the skills that already existed in the nearby gun and jewellery workshops. With the advantage of power from a newly installed gas engine to drive his factory machinery, Alfred was able to develop further his particular specialities—the manufacture of parts from pressed steel and the machining of castings. These ran alongside his production of racing bicycles.

The essence of manufacturing bicycles and motorcycles is the design and building of the tubular frame. Until recent times, the established method was to cut and form the tubes, and then braze them together

Haden 'New Comet' bicycle. circa 1910

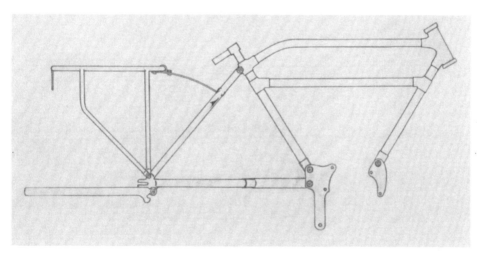

Drawing showing the layout of a Haden motorcycle frame.

using 'connecting pieces' known as frame lugs and fork crowns. The completed frame and front fork would be cleaned and painted, after which the wheels, chain, handlebars, saddle, and other parts would be added. It has generally been accepted that cycle or motorcycle suppliers who do not produce their own frames are not true manufacturers, but only assemblers or importers.

Although production of complete New Comet bicycles and frames

An early Haden ladies loop frame.

appears to have continued until at least 1912, it was in about 1902 that, like several other bicycle manufacturers, Alfred began to explore a new idea that had first appeared in Germany in 1894. This was to fit a small internal combustion engine within the frame of a bicycle. As an established manufacturer of cycle accessories, and with the advantage of his own in-house component manufacturing facility, he was in a strong position to experiment, develop and manufacture new frame designs for motorcycles. Many of his ideas were soon to be adopted by others. He is believed to have produced his first motorcycle in 1903, and although not the first to manufacture a motorcycle in Birmingham, he was certainly one of the more important pioneers. He was known to welcome anyone at the door who had a new idea and would try to realise it for them, or he would expand on other people's patents, but not copy them. He was one of the few who would make things in that way, being not just a clever engineer, but also a go-ahead businessman.

There is a story handed down through the family that on a Saturday morning in about 1905, Alfred was in his office and in response to a knock on the door, received a visitor who had arrived unexpectedly and left his bicycle in the passageway outside. The gentleman explained that he was attempting to build a prototype motorcar and was interested in purchasing a few motorcycle sidecar chassis parts, and anything else that might be of assistance. After looking around the factory, he filled the large basket on the front of his bicycle, paid for the goods and rode off, apparently well-satisfied. His name was Herbert Austin.

From his earlier days, Alfred had always been interested in racing. Although his first motorcycles, produced in 1903,

Small group of employees, Princip Street factory.

South Africa, 1907, success in racing New Comet motorcycles.

Agnes Haden with her own New Comet, 1908.

New Comet Light 2 stroke Lady's model.

were rather primitive by later standards, they were soon developed into first-class reliable machines that successfully competed in local reliability trials. So well were these regarded that a keen motorcyclist of the time, Mr G. Usher, purchased two, and having shipped them home to South Africa, entered practically all the 1907 motorcycle events. He was phenomenally successful, winning many races in that and the following year.

The success of his early designs now led Alfred to trade as New Comet Motors. In 1908 he felt confident enough to launch a complete range of motorcycles, including what was possibly the first ever model designed specifically for ladies, complete with an open frame and fully-enclosed chain guard.

On Saturday 24 April 1909, anxious to prove the reliability of his motorcycles, Alfred took part in the Auto-Cycle Union 125-mile Quarterly Reliability Trial. The route started in Uxbridge and went via Dashwood Hill, Banbury, Bicester, Aylesbury, Berkhamsted, Chesham, and back to Uxbridge. Riding his own New Comet 'Motor Bicycle', Alfred completed the course with only one stoppage, the reason described on the ACU certificate was that he had 'undone and cleaned plug'.

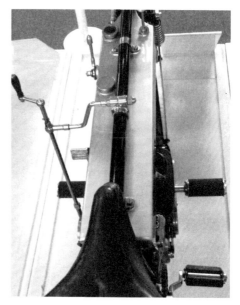

In November 1912, with a now prospering business, a stand was taken at the Third International Cycle, Motorcycle and Cycle Car Exhibition at Olympia, London. Components to build complete frames were clearly an important part of the business and great emphasis was placed on the range of products available, using the slogan 'Everything for Motor Cycles and Sidecars, from a lug to the complete outfit.' The opportunity was taken at this show to launch the Haden three-speed countershaft gearbox, similar to a unit already being

The 1911 New Comet with 500cc Precision engine. The handle on the left is for changing gear (two gears and neutral). This model is on display at the National Motorcycle Museum, Birmingham.

Motorcycle frame components;

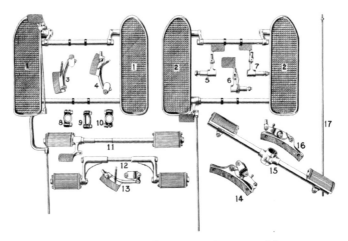

Motorcycle foot plates, foot rests and associated fittings.

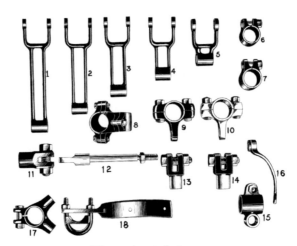

Sidecar chassis fittings.

Haden countershaft gearbox, 1912

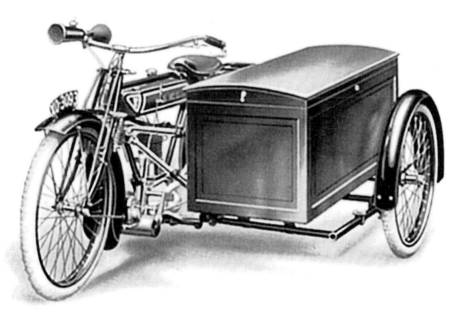

New Comet with sidecar for goods delivery

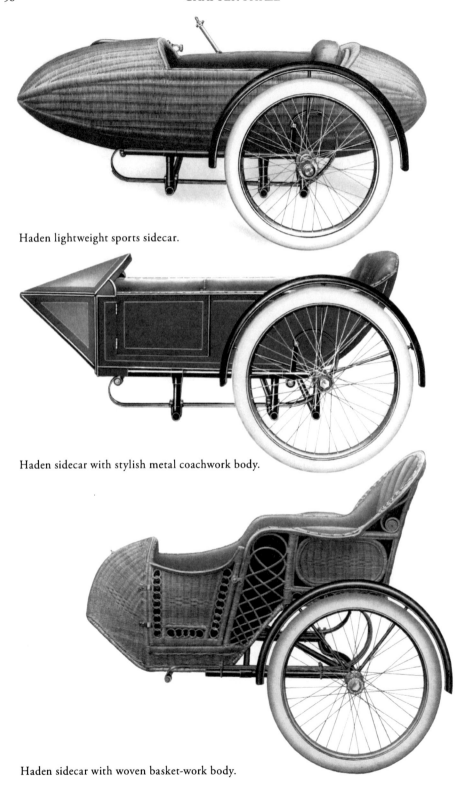

Haden lightweight sports sidecar.

Haden sidecar with stylish metal coachwork body.

Haden sidecar with woven basket-work body.

produced by Sturmey Archer. This type of gearbox was now superseding the more traditional epicyclic hub gear, being more robust and easier to dismantle and repair.

A glance at the 1912 exhibition catalogue suggests that by now many sidecar manufacturers and other pioneers were developing various forms of personal transport to meet the expectations of the increasingly affluent middle classes. Sidecars were built not just to carry passengers but, alternatively, with a flat truck-like body or similar for the commercial delivery of goods. With his wide range of manufacturing capabilities, Alfred was able not only to meet the demand for special chassis parts but also to develop his own sidecar designs that perfectly matched the machine to which they were to be fitted. He had a particular interest in producing a reliable lightweight combination

Hadens' Comet, Colonial model (left hand drive), with Precision engine.

based on his renowned New Comet motorcycle. Amongst the models on offer at that time was the Colonial, designed to cope with overseas road conditions. It was available with, or without, a specially adapted sidecar and featuring an unusual rear brake operated by the left foot on the belt rim.

In 1913 the opportunity arose to acquire the business of the London based motorcycle and engine manufacturer Regal Green. The assets were purchased and production transferred to Birmingham, where Alfred had recently moved to larger premises further along Princip Street at number forty-four. An imposing frontage with first floor offices gave a new standing to the company and prospects for ongoing expansion were looking very favourable.

The Regal Green assets included some special purpose machinery which Alfred now employed in the manufacture of a new engine, the design of which he had been working on for several years. This single-cylinder, 293cc, two-stroke engine had several special features. In particular it had a rather distinctive shape of cylinder featuring a reduction in the size of the radiating fins that ran from top to bottom in wedge formation and, innovatively, a pair of cast-iron flywheels mounted inside the crankcase. Alfred named this his Climax engine and it remained

Alfred with his children on a New Comet Combination, 1913. The sidecar is mounted on the right hand side for continental use.

in production for many years. This was the engine that he later used so successfully in the 1920 and 1921 TT Races, to be described later.

It was at about this time that Alfred introduced and patented his own special lubrication system, which fed oil directly into the two-stroke engine crankcase via a sight-feed pump.

The New Comet with Haden Climax engine and Albion gearbox.

The New Comet with Haden Climax engine and Albion gearbox.

Office staff at Princip Street factory.

A section of the motorcycle assembly department.

Motorcycle side-cars being loaded for delivery to the railway station by horse-drawn flat wagon.

MOTOR CYCLES. 122

Name of Motor Cycle.	Maker's Horse-power.	No. of Cyls.	Bore and Stroke, m/m.	Type.	Motor Cycles manufactured in the year where List Price is quoted.				
					1917	1916	1915	1914	1913
					£	£	£	£	£
N.U.T. (contd.) (J.A.P. Engine)	3½	2	70 × 64½	3 Sp CcB CS V OH	*	*	72¾	...	...
	3½	2	70 × 64½	Fx B V	*	*	59½	...	...
	3½	2	70 × 64½	3 Sp CcB CS V	*	*	69½	...	...
	3½	2	70 × 64½	Fx B V	*	*	56¼	...	...
	6	2	76 × 85	3 Sp CcB CS V	*	*	80½	...	...
	6	2	76 × 85	Fx B V	*	*	67¼	...	...
	8	2	85½ × 85	3 Sp CcB CS V	*	*	82¾	...	...
New Comet (British) A. H. Haden	2¼	1	62 × 70	...	...	26½	25	...	...
	2¾	1	75 × 79	...	...	36¼	33	...	...
	2	1	65 × 60	...	..	31⅛	29	...	...
	3½	1	85 × 88	...	...	46⅛	42	...	...
	6	2	76 × 85	...	...	75¾	68½	...	...
New Hudson (British) The New Hudson Cycle Co., Ltd.	2¼	1	62 × 70	TS	*	42	40	38	...
	4	1	85 × 88	3 Sp	*	65	63	57½	57½
	6	2	76 × 85	3 Sp	*	92¾	92¾	88¼	84
New Imperial (British) New Imperial Cycles, Ltd.	2¾	1	70 × 76	2 Sp CcB CS	41	36¾	32½	32½	32½
	2¾	1	70 × 76	2 Sp K	48¼	43	37¾	37¾	...
(Lady's)	2¾	1	70 × 76	2 Sp K	50⅞	45⅛	43	43	...
New Ryder (British) New Ryder Motor Cycle Co., Ltd. (J.A.P. Engine)	2½	1	70 × 70	TS	33	28¾	27¼	26¼	...
	2½	1	70 × 76	2 Sp CS	37½	34⅝	33¼	...	...
Norton (British) Norton Motors, Ltd.	4	1	82 × 120	3 Sp C K	*	68⅞	63½	...	...
	4	1	82 × 120	3 Sp CcB K	*	67⅞	64½	...	...

For Notes and References see page 101.

Motorcycle production, Grace's Guide 1913–1917.

With the dark clouds of the First World War rapidly approaching, a degree of uncertainty was about to cause many changes. A major part of the manufacturing industry in the West Midlands began the process of changing over to the production of armaments and associated wartime items. As it happened, Alfred was well-placed, and although motorcycle production was reduced, orders for military sidecars and chassis flowed in, not just from the British War office but also from Russian military forces.

Many consignments despatched to the Imperial Russian Army never reached their destination, the ships carrying them having been sunk in the North Sea by the German Navy. The business was prospering and, by 1915, Alfred was able to move with his growing family to a substantial neo-Georgian house in the leafy suburbs of Erdington, on the outskirts of the city.

Alfred's new home in Erdington 1915.

As the war came to a close, Alfred began to look for new ideas. There was an obvious interest in invalid carriages for injured soldiers and a prototype was produced. Later, many component parts designed for orthopaedic aids were developed and the connection with that industry continued right through until 2002.

Haden invalid tricycle

Alfred appears to have had a particular interest in overseas markets and is known to have travelled on business to both France and Italy. With an agent appointed in France, he was now confident enough to refer to his business principally as that of a motorcycle manufacturer. By 1919 he had revived and redeveloped the New Comet, and with the enthusiastic support of his son Sidney, embarked on a plan to prove the reliability and performance of his improved design by taking part in several important time trials and races.

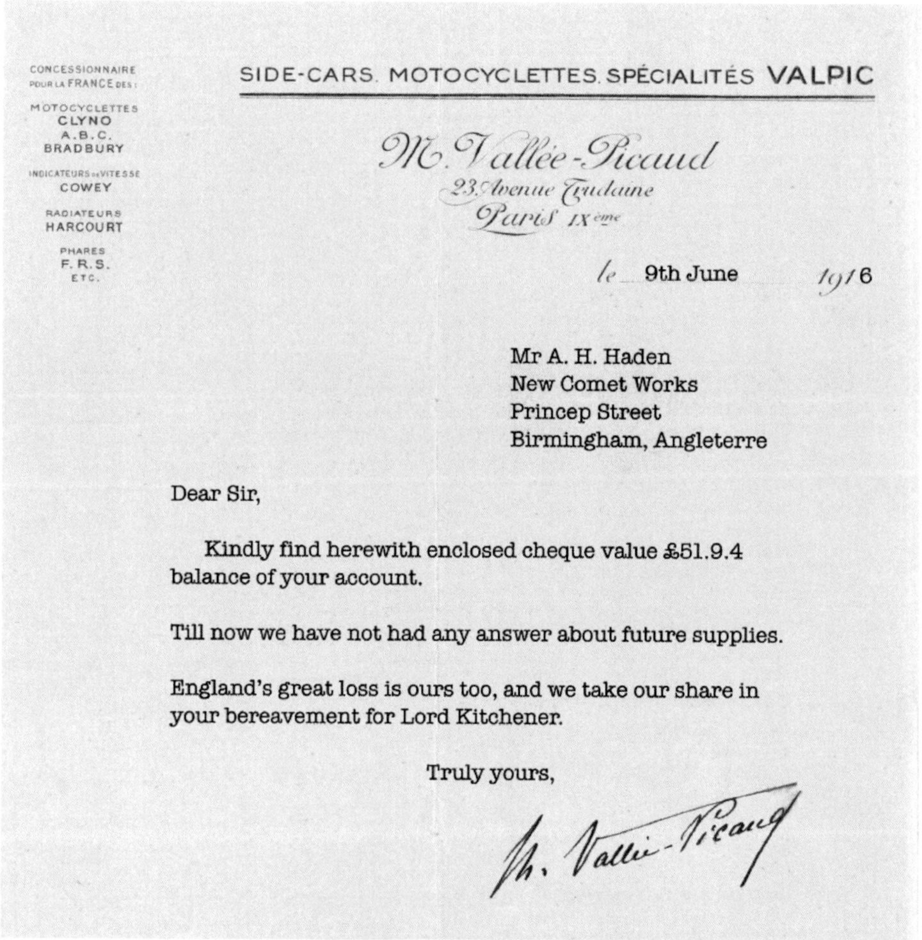

CONCESSIONNAIRE
POUR LA FRANCE DES :

MOTOCYCLETTES
CLYNO
A.B.C.
BRADBURY

INDICATEURS DE VITESSE
COWEY

RADIATEURS
HARCOURT

PHARES
F.R.S.
ETC.

SIDE-CARS. MOTOCYCLETTES. SPÉCIALITÉS **VALPIC**

M. Vallée-Picaud
23 Avenue Trudaine
Paris IX ème

le 9th June *1916*

Mr A. H. Haden
New Comet Works
Princep Street
Birmingham, Angleterre

Dear Sir,

Kindly find herewith enclosed cheque value £51.9.4 balance of your account.

Till now we have not had any answer about future supplies.

England's great loss is ours too, and we take our share in your bereavement for Lord Kitchener.

Truly yours,

Ph. Vallée-Picaud

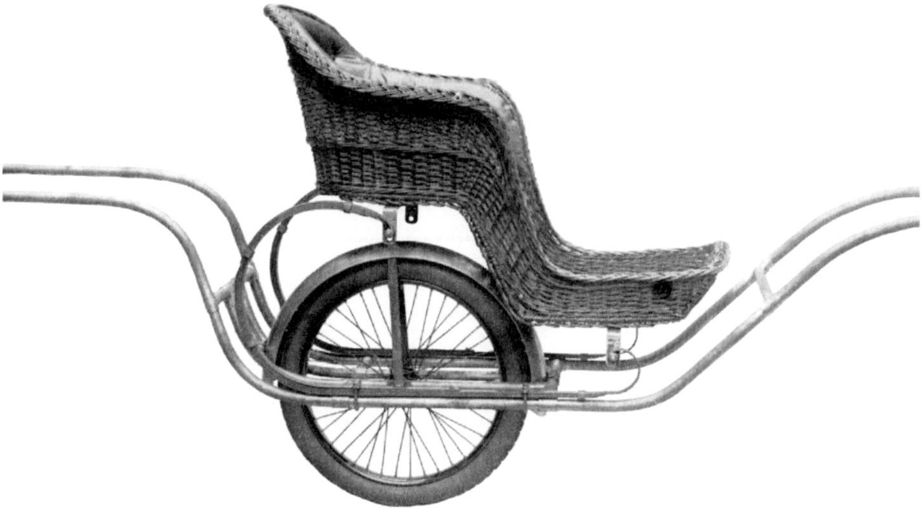

Haden rickshaw

Alfred at the works of A Baratelli & Co in Milan. circa 1912.

Group of motorcycle manufacturers at the Isle of Man TT Races 1921. (Alfred is second from right with moustache.)

Sidney Haden astride the works entered New Comet 293cc two-stroke ready for the 1920 Junior TT Race.

Governor's Bridge 14 June 1921 Junior TT Race. Sidney Haden on New Comet 293cc TS

Isle of Mann TT Races 1920–21

The famous Isle of Man TT Races had been suspended during the war but by 1920 there was sufficient interest to make a re-start. There was a logistical problem in getting all the competitors and officials across the Irish Sea because of a severe shortage of ships. Petrol was in short supply and the ACU insisted on a minimum of thirty entrants for each race. A new addition for the 1920 event was a race for 250cc machines to be run concurrently with the 350cc Junior, to be called the Lightweight TT. This fitted perfectly with Alfred's development strategy and so he

TT1920 Junior TT Results TT 1920			
Posn	No	Competitor	Machine
1	0	Cyril Williams	AJS
2	0	J. A. Watson-Bourne	Blackburne
3	0	J. S. Holroyd	Blackburne
4	0	R. O. Clarke	Levis
5	0	E. Longden	DOT
6	0	R. W. Loughton	Douglas
7	0	Gus Kuhn	Levis
8	0	H. V. Prescott	AJS
9	0	F. W. Applebee	Levis
10	**0**	**S. H. Haden**	**New Comet**
11	0	P. G. Dallison	Ivy
DNF	0	A. H. Alexander	Douglas
DNF	0	Howard R Davies	AJS
DNF	0	P. J. Enticknapp	Blackburne
DNF	0	H. F. Harris	AJS
DNF	0	A. F. Houlberg	Wooler
DNF	0	S. A. Marks	Diamond
DNF	0	A. Milner	Diamond
DNF	0	P. Pike	Diamond
DNF	0	N. C. Sclater	Aurora
DNF	0	Tom Sheard	AJS
DNF	0	O. Wade	AJS
DNF	0	Eric Williams	AJS
DNF	0	A. E. Wills	Douglas

Official results of 14 June 1920 Junior TT Race.

entered one of his New Comet motorcycles complete with his own Climax engine.

By the standard of the day, the Manx roads were on the whole fairly primitive—almost the whole of the TT course was either rolled earth and stone or, in the mountain section, just old cart tracks. Riders had to complete five laps, a total distance of 189 miles, and in order to be well-placed they had to average in the region of 50 m.p.h. It was decided that Alfred's second son, Sidney, would take part riding a sports version of the standard 293cc twin-stroke New Comet. The race went very well, the reliability of the machine being proved beyond question. Sidney finished comfortably in tenth position out of twenty-four starters, having reportedly pulled into the pits at the end of every lap for a snack. The Haden New Comet was the only standard model entered in the TT races that year to complete the course.

Anxious to prove further the reliability and performance of his machines, Alfred took his standard 293cc two-stroke engined New Comet to Brooklands. This time with a sidecar fitted, he was hoping to set new

THE AUTO-CYCLE UNION.

CERTIFICATE OF RECORD.

This is to Certify that a claim to the RECORD of

5 hours Class B with Sidecar.

350 c.c at 40.12 m.p.h

has been recognised by the **AUTO-CYCLE UNION** for the performance of

M. J. J. Newey.

in driving a 2¾ h.p. New Comet

at Brooklands   on   28th April   1921

Chairman, Competitions Committee.

Date issued 10th November 1921.

Secretary:

No. 267

83 PALL MALL,
LONDON, S.W.1.

records. At that time, Brooklands was used not just for racing but also for road testing of individual cars and motorcycles by their manufacturers, monitored by the ACU for record purposes. The steeply-banked track had a reputation for being rather dangerous. It was said that in the event of a bad accident, the only medical assistance was a man with a shovel. It was on 28 April 1921 that the New Comet set off, this time ridden by

Mr J. T. Newey who was pleased to report to Alfred that:

> . . . carrying twenty-one stone and with complete success our New
> Comet secured world's records at Brooklands beating all previous
> records in the 350cc class for four hours, five hours and two hundred
> miles equal to over 40 m.p.h. continuous running without any
> organisation or staff.

In June 1921, no doubt full of enthusiasm for further successes, the
Haden team returned to the Isle of Man, together with Alfred's twin
sons, Denis and Donald. They were aged only nine and described on this
occasion as junior mechanics so as to allow them entry into the reserved
cage in the pits. During a practice run there was some concern that Sidney
may have broken down, but he was eventually spotted in the distance
returning safely, explaining that he had stopped halfway round to have
a cigarette. There was much stronger competition to face that year, but
the New Comet, powered by the Haden Climax engine, again showed
its reliability, finishing twenty-fourth out of fifty-eight starters, of whom
only thirty-eight finished.

Only a month later, Alfred sent his rider Mr Newey back to Brooklands,
again with a New Comet Combination. On 12 July, he was awarded an
ACU certificate, having secured a new endurance record with the same
outfit, this time for six hours at an average speed of 39.05 m.p.h. The
company's sales literature of that time states that these records were
recognised as marking an extraordinary advance in two-stroke engine
design. The technical excellence of the Haden Climax engine had at
last been recognised, and with strongly supportive articles in the trade
magazines and, as always, his ability to improve, Alfred appears to have
continued to prosper.

Later that year, having purchased a French-built Darracq motorcar,
Alfred set off with his family on board to Llandudno for the weekend,
stopping off after about forty miles at the Weston Arms Hotel for coffee.
He had been driving with his chauffeur/mechanic alongside and was
puzzled as to why the car appeared to be so slow. He was, of course, only
ever used to driving motorcycles, which in those days often only had two
forward gears at most. His chauffeur had to point out to him that this

Alfred driving his Darracq motor-car.

Motorcycle Exhibition, Bingley Hall, Birmingham 1923.

new car actually had four forward gears as well as a reverse. At that time, every summer Alfred took a house adjacent to Anne Hathaway's cottage in Stratford-upon-Avon, where his growing family could enjoy the delights of that area, while he could still motor to his office every day.

The 1920s had ushered in what many called the Golden Age of motorcycling. At the 1919 London Olympia show, there were at least fifty new manufacturers and within two years this had risen to over a hundred. However, because of the increased availability of small family cars at very low prices—such as the Austin Seven which was re-launched on 21 July 1922—competition became intense, and many of the smaller motorcycle manufacturers who did not have the cost advantage of large-scale production methods, or new innovative ideas, were soon to disappear.

In 1923, as a challenge no doubt to the expanding motorcar industry, Alfred launched an improved version of his New Comet Light Touring Combination at an exhibition at Bingley Hall, Birmingham. This machine, complete with his Climax engine, was expressly designed as a low cost passenger vehicle to provide an ideal and economic form of motoring, not just for 'about town' use, but also for touring. The special feature of his Climax engine—its internal flywheels located inside the crankcase directly underneath the cylinder block—led him to market this model as 'the machine with the heart in the right place'.

In 1925 Alfred's eldest son, Alf, left the family business, emigrating to New Zealand. He settled in Christchurch and for a number of years successfully managed a motorcycle and motorcar distribution company. He imported British bikes, including some New Comets, a few of which are known to still survive there today. With his inherited interest in engineering, Alf took up flying as a hobby and was a founder member and vice captain of the Mid-Canterbury Aero Club, established in 1928.

Meanwhile, back in England, as the Great Depression worsened, Alfred was having difficulty in keeping the business afloat. Even though he reduced his prices, orders for his beloved New Comet were drying up and he was increasingly having to rely on sales of components in a reducing market. In 1928 the decision was made to cease motorcycle production. The introduction of a new 172cc two-stroke Super Sports model had not been a success and the struggle to manage the business was having an effect on Alfred's health. Relationships within the family at home were now becoming strained. In order to pay off debts, the company of A. H. Haden Ltd. was dissolved on 16 May 1930. Somehow or other, the principal assets were retained by the family and part of the premises was let out.

Trading now as A. H. Haden Co., an attempt to restart motorcycle production was made, first with the revival of the 172cc Super Sports, and then a new 196cc version. But this was not successful and factory production was again reduced to cycle and motorcycle fittings. It was not until Alfred's twin sons, Denis and Donald (father of the author), took control in 1938 that the business started to prosper once more.

Victor, Alfred's eldest son by his second marriage, set up a small radio repair business in part of the Princip Street factory, but this was not fruitful. He was educated at the King Edward VI Foundation School in Birmingham (later located in Edgbaston), where among his contemporaries he was able to count Enoch Powell and the atom spy Alan Nunn May. Later, at university he was awarded a PhD and went on to become a highly respected consultant engineer, engaged in a senior position at the Royal Dutch Shell Group.

It was around this time that Alfred retired from the business, and his much-loved daughter Mildred left home. It was said in the family that he was heartbroken to lose her, for after training to a high level in speech and drama and converting to Catholicism, Mildred entered a Dominican

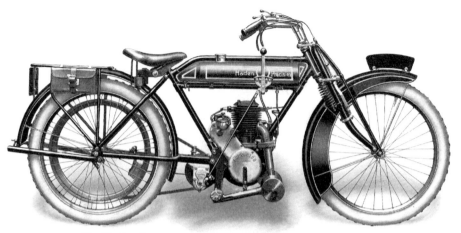

The Haden Precision with Precision engine and Albion gearbox.

The (Haden) Regal Precision fitted with 3½ Villiers Free engine.

The (Haden) Planet, with Precision engine.

convent, very much against her parents' wishes. A strong-minded woman, she was a teacher all her working life and was twice a headmistress. In her later years, she became the first woman to teach at Oscott Seminary College, when the Bishop of Birmingham invited her to give elocution instruction to the Jesuit novices, a duty she fulfilled with great dedication and perseverance. Priests who received instruction from Sister Mildred subsequently described the lessons as instructive, invigorating and novel. She often had them doing yoga on the floor. Always very loyal to her family, when she later retired to the Dominican convent in Stone, Staffordshire, Mildred insisted that the sisters use Haden electric kettles as manufactured by her brother Denis—a business to be described in the later pages of this book.

Alfred died on 30 December 1940 following an unfortunate accident. He fell off his bicycle while returning home one evening from his local hostelry, a sad end for a man who had been a pioneer in the development of the British motorcycle industry. Although he was not a major manufacturer, with his sharp brain, hard work and innovative ideas, he had undoubtedly made an important contribution towards early motorcycle design.

The Win-Precision, manufactured by A. H. Haden Ltd.

There are at least five Haden New Comet motorcycles still in existence, two in the UK and three in New Zealand. There may be more that are not known to the author. Other motorcycle models made by Alfred Haden, but sold under different brand names, include Haden's Comet, Precision, Haden Precision, Regal Precision, The Win Precision and The Planet. The Victoria 1912 motorcycle with a Precision engine has a frame that is identical to other Haden models.

The Haden Climax Motorcycle Engine

The story of Alfred's achievements would not be complete without a careful record of the features and advantages of the engine that he designed and developed himself. The following extract from a New Comet sales brochure published in 1921 is in his own words:

> The Climax two-stroke engine is not a new creation, nor a copy of any existing design. Designed in 1913 after experimental and research work extending over ten years, the manufacture was commenced shortly before the outbreak of war in 1914. The results obtained by private owners of these engines during five years have been remarkable. A low petrol consumption, sustained power over long distances and the almost entire absence of wear on the working parts.

Haden Climax engine 293cc two stroke.

The Climax engine—70mm bore, by 76mm stroke (293cc) 2½ h.p.—is the two-stroke in its simplest form, working on the three port system. The exhaust leaves the cylinder by a straight tube to the aluminium silencer. The incoming charge taking an upward direction and the exhausted gases a nearly downward one, without deflection.

The C.A.V. Magneto is driven by ½ inch by ⅛ inch chain, entirely enclosed. The connecting rod big end has roller bearing, the small end and side bearings, phosphor bronze of large diameter and length. Well thought out arrangements are made for collecting and distributing of the separated oil.

In two important matters the manufacturers depart from the more usual two-stroke design:

FIRST. Though the engine is well-balanced at normal speed, the designers realising that it is impracticable to accomplish perfect balancing with a single cylinder internal combustion engine, have utilised the weight of the flywheels, centrally disposed to absorb the stresses due to imperfect balance and to relieve the frame and transmission of the effect of rapid shocks.

Central in the machine, directly under and in line with the reciprocating parts, the flywheels form an integral part of the unit, performing their function before the transmission of power to the road wheel commences. The makers consider the results obtained by this combination—the two-stroke and the inside flywheels—the smoothness of the transmission and the peculiar hold on the road under the worst conditions have more than justified the adoption of this design.

SECOND. Not only have the makers dealt with the imperfect balance of the single cylinder machine at varying speeds, but have tackled the problem of the inefficiency of the two-stroke under varying loads in a unique and interesting way.

In the Climax engine the design permits of advantage being taken of the elasticity of the gases to vary the velocity of the incoming charge within certain useful speeds. This self-regulation of the tension of the gases in the crankcase, other than by control of the volume, is a factor to which the makers attach the utmost importance and to which they attributed the very low petrol consumption and the absence of overheating. Perhaps 80 per cent of the riding is comparatively easy going, but fuel needlessly consumed means heat losses needlessly incurred, and a lowering of power and usefulness of the machine.

The Climax engine is not a cheap two-stroke. The least observant will see that cheapness of production has not influenced the design or controlled the choice of the materials used. It is manufactured under the direct supervision of the designers.

Every engine is tested on the road under ordinary touring conditions, the parts are standardized and every care is taken that the make and finish of these engines should be of the very highest quality.

(AHH 1921)

WHAT THE PRESS SAYS

THE most interesting feature is undoubtedly the engine, which is one with which Mr Haden has been experimenting for some considerable time. The cylinder is the usual three-port type, and has a bore and stroke of 70mm by 76mm respectively, giving a capacity of 293cc. A compression release valve is situated in the head and releases gasses into the open air. A rather distinctive shape of cylinder has been involved by reducing the size of the radiating fins from top to bottom in wedge formation. Two-stroke engines, with few exceptions, are constructed with external fly-wheels, but in the New Comet a pair of cast-iron fly-wheels are enclosed within the crankcase. The frame is of sturdy construction, and, it is claimed, is sufficiently strong for occasional light side car work.

Motor Cycling

MR HADEN has shown commendable activity in initiating many of those later improvements in the motor cycle which constitutes so noteworthy a feature of his work. The questions of lightness, speed, constructional solidity, and reliability, have all been satisfactorily dealt with in the making of the motor cycles identified with his name and they can fairly claim to be unexcelled upon any of these essential points.

The Business World

FOUNDED in 1869, the business of Mr A. H. Haden can be fairly termed a pioneer undertaking, for it was in that year that the first 'velocipede' races were run at the Crystal Palace and general public interest in cycling may be regarded as dating. Having kept pace with the whole advance of the cycle trade this house, as might well be expected, was not slow to perceive the great possibilities foreshadowed by the application of self-propulsion to vehicles of the bicycle type; and when the motorcycle became an accomplished fact the name of Haden was speedily found among those associated with its production and improvement. Some very notable results have followed, and it is not too much to say that this firm's 'New Comet' Motor Cycles – British made and of splendid construction throughout – represent an unsurpassed standard of excellence in design, durability and strength. Signal competitive triumphs stand to their credit, and notably in South Africa, where their successes have been phenomenal; while as far as the home trade is concerned it is claimed that the Haden A1 Frame, with dropped top-rail and two-way head, revolutionised the motor-cycle business in this country. The 'New Comet' Motor Cycles are holding their own so well in all markets that it would be a work of supererogation to enlarge upon the points of merit that have brought them into such high favour. The many who know them will require no better proof of their worth than actual experience has supplied.

Review of Commerce

John Haden's Personal Experience of Owning and Riding a New Comet Motorcycle

My particular vehicle is a 1921 single speed edition, promoted originally for 'good performance', with the option of adding a clutch and gearbox for journeys less sporting in nature, or trips involving steeper gradients such as may be found in hilly or mountainous areas. It is fitted with a single cylinder 269cc Villiers mark 3 engine.

OE1115 was consigned to a garden shed in 1928 when *Stop* signs, *Give Way* signs and traffic lights had sprung up all over the country, particularly in urban areas. These caused some distress

John Haden's 1921 restored New Comet with 269cc Villiers mark 3 engine.

to all single speed owner/riders and it became compulsory to slow right down—or worse still, stop. Normally, of course, one only did this at either the completion of a journey or for the process of taking on fuel (for either bike or rider).

Stopping was not really the problem, however; starting again was the pain as it was necessary to push the bike with the decompression lever held open until a suitable speed would enable the lever to be released, shutting the valve and encouraging the engine to roar into life. This trick is relatively easy on a favourable slope and very easy on a hill, but on level ground or a gently upward incline is really quite hard work (and uphill well-nigh impossible).

All these facts raced through my mind on the very first event I undertook after years of planning, restoration, training, tuning, expense and eventually obtaining the appropriate licence. I was therefore very grateful [May 1998] for the helpful push start from the dignitaries of the VMCC [Vintage Motor Cycle Club] and the Mayoress of Burton-upon-Trent.

Less than two miles after the start (approaching the A50 on the A444 on the north side of the old Burton–Trent Bridge) I observed 300 yards of stationary vehicles ahead. This particular bridge was always a bottleneck on a Sunday when amateur footballers, rowers, and goers-out-to-lunch mingled with those good souls who had been paying their respects to their departed loved ones at the municipal cemetery (known locally as the Dead Centre of Burton).

The choice was clear; riding up the outside of the line would cause problems at the junction where every other car wished to make a right turn. The prescribed route for the event demanded that I should go straight on so the only choice was to ignore all social etiquette and ride up the inside gutter which appeared to be clear for most of the way. So far, so good. As the junction got even closer, every yard was a milestone, as the terrain could now be described as a gentle slope. I was undeterred, appreciating the fact that all my training had not been wasted; by juggling the air and mixture levels, sliding the ignition lever to maximum 'retard', progress was made at a relatively safe 10 m.p.h. But the traffic lights continued to make their red commands, and my brakes were basically decorative; would the lights change to green to coincide with my arrival?

Imagine my surprise when a police constable, obviously concerned about the state of the traffic, stepped out into 'my' gutter in order to obtain a better view of the tailback! It was bad enough juggling the levers. Now I had to decide whether to risk taking out the constable as well as gambling on the lights.

It was my lucky day. The constable retreated, the lights changed, nobody turned left and I made it over the junction towards Newton Solney.

Completing the run some time later, I had the pleasure of receiving an award for best two-stroke from Titch Allen (founder of the VMCC) who congratulated me on the state of the bike. There was a particular feature that caught his attention—the multi-hole mounting plates for optional engines and gearboxes—which he believed to be unique to the New Comet marque.

That was only the start. Now, a few years later, I can testify that every ride on a single speeder has its 'will it/won't it' moments—sometimes a few too many perhaps. But I have lived to tell the tale and have recently fitted a contemporary (to the year 1921) three-speed Albion gearbox and clutch which should enable lots more fun to be had with a somewhat less cavalier approach to junctions and other highway impedimenta.

Now, about those brakes . . . !

Left, Donald
W. Haden.

Right, Denis
H. Haden.

CHAPTER FOUR
A New Beginning: A New Generation Takes Charge 1938–1961

The future is unknowable, but the past should give us hope.
(Winston Churchill, *A History of the English-speaking Peoples*)

On taking over their father's business in 1938, twin brothers Denis and Donald (father of the author) looked at how they might improve matters, and first decided to move from 44 Princip Street to a more practical site on the other side of the city. The Princip Street factory was sold to the neighbouring business of M. A. Lloyd and Son and new premises purchased in Little Edward Street, Bordesley. The factory had previously been occupied by Donald Edward (Birmingham) Ltd. who were wire drawers. Previous to that it had been a button-making workshop, complete with stables and some small dwellings for the workers. Horses fetched the bones for making the buttons from the local slaughterhouse and these were tipped into the yard for sorting and cleaning before being taken into the workshop for turning, drilling and polishing. Although by modern standards some of the buildings were in a somewhat dilapidated state, they were soon made more habitable. Open yards were covered in to house some of the machinery, press tools and other equipment which was being brought over from Princip Street, and the stables were converted into a tool room.

As a result of their existing contacts with the nearby BSA bicycle factory in Small Heath, the two brothers, trading now as Haden Bros., embarked on the manufacture of wartime products. These were mainly

Earls Court Cycle and Motorcycle Show circa 1953.

parts for tanks which they made as subcontractors to BSA who had themselves switched from bicycles to armament production. Using their skills in welding, tube bending, metal forming, and press tool making, the brothers developed a particular skill in cutting and forming armour-plated steel. Although there is no record of the precise products made, there is a story handed down that one weekend an American military vehicle was brought to the factory so that a prototype upright exhaust pipe could be fabricated and fitted. This design enabled vehicles so equipped to be driven safely through shallow waters from their landing craft during the Normandy landing in France. At this stage of development only about twenty-five people were employed. Denis managed production whilst Donald dealt with the commercial arrangements. Everyone employed worked very much as a team, doing whatever might be necessary and working long hours in order to get the orders out on time.

Indeed, the brothers worked extremely hard during the war, and even though they were close to the heavily-bombed major railway goods yard in Lawley Street, they did not suffer any serious damage to their factory.

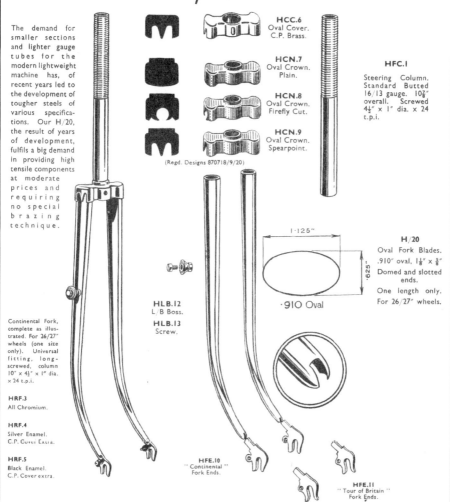

LIGHTWEIGHT "CONTINENTAL" FORK

IN OUR SPECIAL H/20 HIGH TENSILE STEEL

The demand for smaller sections and lighter gauge tubes for the modern lightweight machine has, of recent years led to the development of tougher steels of various specifications. Our H/20, the result of years of development, fulfils a big demand in providing high tensile components at moderate prices and requiring no special brazing technique.

HCC.6
Oval Cover.
C.P. Brass.

HCN.7
Oval Crown.
Plain.

HCN.8
Oval Crown.
Firefly Cut.

HCN.9
Oval Crown.
Spearpoint.

(Regd. Designs 870718/9/20)

HFC.1

Steering Column.
Standard Butted
16/13 gauge. 10⅞"
overall. Screwed
4½" x 1" dia. x 24
t.p.i.

1·125"

·625"

H/20
Oval Fork Blades.
.910" oval, 1⅛" x ⅞"
Domed and slotted
ends.
One length only.
For 26/27" wheels.

·910 Oval

HLB.12
L/B Boss.

HLB.13
Screw.

Continental Fork,
complete as illus-
trated. For 26/27"
wheels (one size
only). Universal
fitting, long-
screwed, column
10" x 4½" x 1" dia.
x 24 t.p.i.

HRF.3
All Chromium.

HRF.4
Silver Enamel.
C.P. Cover Extra.

HRF.5
Black Enamel.
C.P. Cover extra.

HFE.10
"Continental"
Fork Ends.

HFE.11
"Tour of Britain"
Fork Ends.

Warranty

List No. 54   Page 2

LIGHTWEIGHT
CYCLE FRAME LUG SETS
IN 17 GAUGE HIGH GRADE STEEL

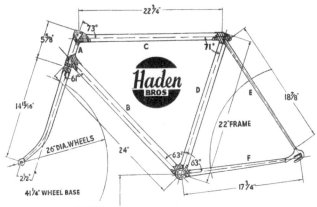

GENT'S ROAD RACING CYCLES
"FIREFLY" LIGHTWEIGHT FRAME
TYPICAL LAYOUT FOR N/R7 SET

FRAME SIZE	TUBE LENGTHS with allowance for mitreing					
	A	B	C	D	E	F
22 inch ...	$5\frac{5}{8}''$	$22\frac{7}{8}''$	$21\frac{7}{8}''$	$21\frac{5}{16}''$	$18\frac{1}{8}''$	$14\frac{7}{8}''$
Tube sizes ...	$1\frac{1}{4}''$ dia.	$1\frac{1}{8}''$ dia.	$1''$ dia.	$1\frac{1}{8}''$ dia.	$\frac{7}{8}'' - \frac{13}{16}''$ dia. tapered	$\frac{7}{8}'' - \frac{9}{16}''$ dia. tapered and fluted

SET No. N/R7
NO RACE

HTL.101
Top Head Lug
$1\frac{1}{4}'' \times 1'' \times 73°$

HSL.103
Seat Lug
$1\frac{1}{8}'' \times 1'' \times 71°$
(or with 3/16" Spigots)

HBL.102
Bottom Head Lug
$1\frac{1}{4}'' \times 1\frac{1}{8}'' \times 61°$

HBS.104
Bottom Bracket Shell
$1\frac{1}{8}'' \times 1\frac{1}{8}'' \times \frac{7}{8}'' \times 1\frac{1}{4}''$ C.L.
$\times 63° \times 63°$ Cotterless
V Pattern
(Malleable)

ADDITIONS TO "FIREFLY" RANGE GENT'S AND LADIES'
"Firefly" sets are also available in the following alternative angles :—

Gent's Set No. NR/8, Firefly Cutaway.
HTL.117 Top Head Lug, $1\frac{1}{4}'' \times 1'' \times 72°$
HBL.118 Bottom Head Lug, $1\frac{1}{4}'' \times 1\frac{1}{8}'' \times 61°$
HSL.119 Seat Lug, $1\frac{1}{8}'' \times 1'' \times 72°$
HBS.120 Bottom Bracket Shell,
$1\frac{1}{8}'' \times 1\frac{1}{8}'' \times \frac{7}{8}'' \times 61° \times 64°$

Gent's Set No. NR/9, Firefly Cutaway.
HTL.121 Top Head Lug, $1\frac{1}{4}'' \times 1'' \times 69°$
HBL.122 Bottom Head Lug, $1\frac{1}{4}'' \times 1\frac{1}{8}'' \times 64°$
HSL.123 Seat Lug, $1\frac{1}{8}'' \times 1'' \times 69°$
HBS.124 Bottom Bracket Shell,
$1\frac{1}{8}'' \times 1\frac{1}{8}'' \times \frac{7}{8}'' \times 64° \times 61°$

Ladies' Set No. NR/10, Firefly Cutaway.
HTL.125 Top Head Lug, $1\frac{1}{4}'' \times \frac{7}{8}'' \times 69°$
HBL.122 Bottom Head Lug, $1\frac{1}{4}'' \times 1\frac{1}{8}'' \times 64°$
HSL.127 Seat Lug, $1\frac{1}{8}''$ Plain, Flush Ears. No Spigots.
HLL.128 Loop Lug, $1\frac{1}{4}'' \times \frac{7}{8}'' \times 69°$ Plain.
HBS.124 Bottom Bracket Shell,
$1\frac{1}{8}'' \times 1\frac{1}{8}'' \times \frac{7}{8}'' \times 64° \times 61°$

All seat lugs can be fitted with 3/16" Spigots to order.

List No. 54   Page 3

Many nights were spent on fire watch looking for small incendiary bombs that the Luftwaffe dropped in huge numbers. One night some of these started a fire that destroyed the adjoining block of Victorian back-to-back houses at the rear of the factory, providing an opportunity for the company later to acquire extra land. In 1952 the factory was expanded and new modern offices were built fronting Westley Street, befitting the now prospering business. The hard work of the war years was showing results and both brothers were able to move to larger houses and send their children away for private education.

As with many businesses deeply involved in the war effort, as hostilities drew to a close there was much discussion as to what opportunities there were to return to the manufacture of traditional or new products. Clearly, there would be a market for cycle frame parts, a speciality in which the Haden company was well-versed. Several patents were taken out relating to cycle handlebar stems, and tooling was produced so as to extend considerably the company's range of cycle frame lugs and fork crowns. These parts were to become the mainstay of factory production and sales through until the late 1980s.

Hadens had, for several years, been a supplier of bicycle frame parts to BSA, a local company that historically manufactured guns in wartime and bicycles and motorcycles in peacetime. There was a close working relationship between the two companies, and as bicycle production was resumed, orders from BSA became of paramount importance. Unfortunately, the BSA cycle division was sold to Raleigh in 1957 and all production moved to their factory in Nottingham, where they made all their own parts. Notwithstanding increased sales of similar parts to other Midlands-based bicycle factories, the brothers were determined to branch out in other directions. A young buyer who had been at BSA, Jack Daniels, moved to the Rover Car Company where they

Land Rover

were developing the Land Rover four-wheel drive cross-country vehicle for agricultural and military use. Arising from this contact, substantial orders were obtained for the supply of pressed steel and welded assemblies—mostly chassis and small body components. Suspension and engine parts were later supplied for the new P6 saloon cars, and the developing business done with Rover was soon to account for more than 25 per cent of turnover.

The brothers had both played for Erdington Rugby Football Club. Through connections made there during the war, they were able to develop a good working relationship with several Birmingham-based companies who were themselves major suppliers to the motor industry.

The most promising new business opportunity arose from a discussion with Bill Lawley, father of Donald's wife, Eileen. He was a very successful businessman, claiming at one time to have a controlling interest in fifty-two companies, one of them being a small manufacturer of switchgear, Bescol (Electric) Ltd. This company had been built up earlier by a Manchester businessman, Frank Pendergast, who had moved to Birmingham and was related to the Lawleys through marriage. Bescol already made portable electric heating rings for use in the kitchen and it was proposed that by working together, a range of electric kettles and other household electrical appliances could be developed and manufactured.

The essence of an automatic electric kettle is the means by which the electric current can be automatically switched off when the water reaches boiling point. Much thought was given to how a new mechanism could be developed at Bescol which did not conflict with existing patents owned by other manufacturers. The earliest patent that the author has been able to trace is one applied for in July 1944 by a Mr Cecil Annable, a technical consultant acting on behalf of Bescol. But handed-down stories suggest that there may have been an earlier one in the name of a Mr Penny, the accounts manager at Haden Bros., which was developed from ideas discussed with a Mr Yapp, a locally-based engineer and friend of Denis and Donald. The earliest evidence that the author has found of the sale of thermostatically-controlled Bescol kettles, comes from an advertisement in the *Singapore Straits Times* dated 29 December 1946. This suggests that production may have started in late 1944.

Frank Pendergast and Bill Lawley were great friends. As industrialists they liked to employ professional managers to run their companies for them or, as was so common in those days, family members. This was how the brothers Denis and Donald became involved in the management of Bescol, developing that business at the same time as running their own

The Pendergast family, 1916 (Frank is on the far left).

at Westley Street. Bescol was in Parkfield Road and the factories were only about two miles apart. In order to produce some of the kettle parts, the brothers purchased a controlling interest in Adie Manufacturing (Engineers) Ltd., a small injection moulding factory in Dartmouth Street where, using phenol formaldehyde as a raw material, they made the special Bakelite handles, sockets and plugs.

In 1949 Frank Pendergast retired and sold his shares in Bescol to the two brothers. Now as directors, Denis and Donald continued to manage the business on a day-to-day basis, with Bill Lawley as chairman providing some finance, but in the capacity of sleeping partner only. Initially everything went well, sales were good and before long the product range was expanded to include electric fires, convector heaters and related items. Unfortunately, it soon became clear that running two rather different businesses concurrently had its complications and gradually the brothers separated their responsibilities. Denis concentrated more and more on Bescol while Donald continued to run Haden Bros., which was now expanding with new offices and extended factory space. The company was incorporated with limited liability status on 16 March 1954.

Another problem was that Bill Lawley—a forceful character—had a tendency to interfere with the running of operations at Bescol despite, in theory, being only a sleeping partner. This became such an irritation that on 22 May 1957 Donald resigned his directorship. Denis followed suit on 3 April 1958, moving away to set up his own kettle business in Lancaster Street, trading as D. H. Haden Ltd., later moving to Burntwood in Staffordshire. At the same time, Denis sold his interest in Haden Bros. Ltd. to Eileen, wife of Donald, and Bill Lawley bought back the shares in Bescol. This left Donald and his wife Eileen with full control and ownership of Haden Bros. Ltd., the original family business—still principally concerned with the manufacture of components and accessories for the bicycle and motor industries.

Bill Lawley was a charming man who lived in considerable style in a large house in Sutton Coldfield. His chauffeur Howles has always been remembered as probably the only man to ever turn a Rolls-Royce car upside down on the M50 motorway. As with the rest of the family, Bill was a very keen golfer and long-time member of Walmley Golf Club in Sutton Coldfield. The Walmley club house, Springfield, had been the home of the Boultbee Brooks family who had also owned much of the

The Hercules Cycle & Motor Co Ltd.

TELEPHONE
ASTON CROSS 3040 (11 LINES)

CODES
UNIVERSAL TRADE CODE BENTLEYS A.B.C. 5TH EDN.

TELEGRAMS
CYMO, BIRMINGHAM.

Britannia Works, Aston,

LONDON OFFICE & DEPOT
63 b OLD BROMPTON ROAD,
SOUTH KENSINGTON, LONDON S.W.7.
TELEPHONE KENSINGTON 4401 (3 LINES)

Birmingham 6

YOUR REF

OUR REF
B/BC

DATE

9th April 1946

W.E.Lawley Esq.,
Burnside,
Birmingham Road,
WYLDE GREEN.

My dear Bill

      You will, I am sure, be glad to learn that we have fixed up definitely and finally with your friend Withers. In my judgment - and what is of course of infinitely more importance - in the judgment of Sir Edmund, our troubles in the Works look like being over, and your part in this matter is very greatly appreciated by us all.

      Try some time just to tear yourself away from golf and your other pastimes and look in on your working friends about tea-time one afternoon, which as you know is 4 o'clock.

With all regards & again many thanks

Yours as ever

Tiny

land that the course was built on. They were the owners of J. B. Brooks and Co., the well-known Birmingham bicycle saddle makers. Bill Lawley was a founder member of the Senior Golfers' Society and vice president of the Artisan Golfers' Association. Among his many friends he counted the directors of the Hercules Cycle and Motor Company, said at one time to be the largest bicycle manufacturer in the world. By coincidence, their factory in the Aston district of Birmingham occupied the site of an old brewery belonging to the Homer family to whom the Hadens were closely related through marriage.

Left, Joseph P. Lawley, 1845–1916.

Below, seven-plank Lawley coal wagon no. 391.

ALL QUOTATIONS SUBJECT TO THE USUAL STRIKE, LOCK-OUT, ACCIDENT, WAGES & TO ALTERATION IN RAILWAY RATES, &C.,
CLAUSES AND ALL OTHER CONTINGENCIES, AND TO ACCEPTANCE OF SAME BY RETURN OF POST.

All Communications to be addressed to the Firm.

T. A. HAWKINS & SONS,
LIMITED.

Cannock Old Coppice Colliery,

Cheslyn Hay,

TELEPHONE : CHESLYN HAY, 271-272.
TELEGRAMS : HAWKINS COLLIERY, CHESLYN HAY.
PASS. STATION : WYRLEY & CHESLYN HAY, L. M. S. RLY.

via Walsall.

48 Hall Court Crescent
Cannock
Dec 18th 1946

Dear William, Thank you so much for the tobacco you have kindly sent by your good nephew. I was telling him this morning about how you used to come here on your solid tyre bike before 9 oclock in a morning & how you pulled your old firm round again — I have always had a great admiration for your pluck & without any flattery I think you deserve the success you have attained. These sentiments are true & not said because you have so kindly thought of me this Ymas time.

Hope you will have a good time yourself old man.

With kindest remembrance I am
Yours Sincerely
Arthur Jukes

Alderman and Mrs W. E. Lawley.

Wedding of William Lawley to Lillian Wakelin, 1912.

ALL STEEL ADJUSTABLE HANDLEBAR EXTENSIONS

THE "SPEARPOINT" EXTENSION
Specially designed for the Track and Road Racing enthusiast.

" Z 14 " EXTENSION
Standard equipment on the modern Tourist Cycle. As specified by U.S.A. Buyers.

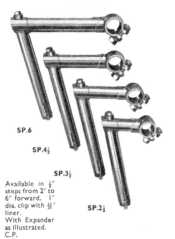

SP.6

SP.4½

SP.3½

Available in ½″ steps from 2″ to 6″ forward. 1″ dia. clip with ⅛″ liner.
With Expander as illustrated. C.P.

SP.2½

Z 14 L
Lug only.

" Z 14 " EXTENSION
With Expander and Clip Bolt as illustrated. Clip reamered ⅞″ only.   Chromium Plated.

MAJOR-TAYLOR "OUTRIGGER"

F.5   F.6   F.7

F.3 F.1 F.4

F.8

F.9

F.1   Expander Bolt, 7¼″ Chrome.
F.2   Expander Cone.
F.3   Saddle Washer, Chrome.
F.4   Oval Lap Filler.
F.5   Back Lap, 6½″
F.6   Extension Tube.
F.7   Steel Spearpoint Clip.
F.8   Clip Bolt, Nut and Washer, Chrome.
F.9   ⅞″ Liner.

F.2

MT.16
Clip only.
Self-Colour.

MT.15
Complete as illustrated.
For ⅞″ or 1″ Bar. C.P.

MT.17
Extension Tube. Self-Colour.
Stem Cap Expander, etc., as Spearpoint.

HADEN BROS. LTD.
WESTLEY STREET · BIRMINGHAM 9 · ENGLAND
Telephone : VICtoria 0461-2   Telegrams : " HADENBRO, BIRMINGHAM "

List No. 54   Page 4

The origin of Bill Lawley's wealth was a small coal merchants business established by his father in the 1890s — J. P. Lawley Ltd. As a young man Bill took control of the business and developed it into what eventually became one of the largest coal distribution companies in the Midlands. At his Cuckoo Wharf depot in Aston he had facilities for loading and unloading canal barges, and at the large Lawley Street goods depot, close to Birmingham city centre, he had his own liveried wagons and private railway sidings. The company delivered coal far and wide, including to Hereford in the west and Wigan Pier in Lancashire.

Another of Bill's successful businesses was Jones & Rooke Ltd. in the Jewellery Quarter, a rolling mill which produced nickel-silver alloy strip for companies around the world.

Even though he had considerable business ability and invested additional capital into Bescol, Bill Lawley was unable to recruit a new managing director who was good enough to take the company forward against the sharp competition now coming from the expanding D. H. Haden Ltd. business. Consequently, trading at Bescol (Electric) Ltd. ceased in 1963. In 1974, for his civic services as a long standing councillor and past mayor of Sutton Coldfield, Bill Lawley was made an alderman of the District Council of Birmingham.

The war years and the period immediately thereafter had been hard for everyone in the family, the problems at Bescol having caused considerable strain. However, as Birmingham grew out of the post-war recession, new opportunities for Haden Bros. began to rapidly unfold. The closure of the BSA cycle factory in nearby Small Heath had been a blow, but there were at least twelve bicycle manufacturers in Birmingham and the Black Country looking to expand their production and therefore requiring frame components—parts that Hadens specialised in manufacturing.

Demand for bicycle handlebar stems was very strong at that time. An important stage in the manufacturing process of these is the brazing together of the various parts. In order to make this as efficient as possible, a Birlec electric conveyor-belt furnace was purchased in 1960 and installed in a special extension to the factory. For the company at that time, this was a major investment, but the process had many applications for other parts they manufactured, including several components supplied to Land Rover.

The 1950s and 1960s were periods of considerable change in all sections of society. For the affluent middle class families, the introduction of cheap mass-produced goods was making life easier. They had fewer children, and with electric washing machines, cookers, Hoovers, irons, and toasters, together with automated gas central heating systems, electric fires and economically priced petrol lawnmowers, they no longer needed to employ live-in domestic servants. With growing prosperity, Donald (the author's father) became the proud owner of a new E-type Jaguar car and family members were able to enjoy extended times in Ireland with their friends. A large house in County Limerick was often taken for Christmas and the summer holidays.

Above, An artist's impression of the main offices and factory at Westley Street, Birmingham.

Left, E-type Jaguar.

Below, Glenwood, Co. Limerick.

CHAPTER FIVE
The Final Years of Manufacturing in Birmingham:
Personal Recollections of the Author

'Things never turn out as you expect, dear boy.'
(Harold Macmillan, Prime Minister 1957–63)

Early Days

After leaving school in 1958 I managed to secure a place as an indentured engineering apprentice with the electric furnace manufacturer AEI Birlec Ltd. They were one of the very few Birmingham companies running such a scheme and had their own separate first-year training school. There were only a limited number of places and there was strong competition for these from school leavers seeking to enter the engineering industry. The managing director, George Tinker, was a personal friend of my maternal grandfather—this may have helped. Apprentices were allowed time off to attend Aston Technical College, where I studied mechanical and electrical engineering. This was the late 1950s and I got the impression that the college syllabuses had not changed much since Victorian times, as we seemed to spend a great deal of time studying the science and workings of steam and gas engines, of which there was an amazing collection in the basement. Never mind, it was all very interesting and the food in the canteen was far better than it had been at school.

I gained some useful practical experience working on the shop floor at AEI Birlec, including machining, welding, and sheet metal work, and spent some time learning the basics of technical drawing and design. In the electric testing section, I remember when we had to try out a new electric cremation furnace, the first to be built in the UK, we burned a coffin shaped box with a sheep carcass inside that the buyer had obtained from the local abattoir.

Joining the Family Business

These were heady days. Britain and her allies had won the war and were still well-placed on the world stage. There was a growing confidence within the country and an expectation and demand from consumers for new products. Birmingham industry was rising to the challenge, and so, in the summer of 1961, I made the decision to leave AEI Birlec and join the family firm. My father insisted, quite rightly, that I spend the first twelve months in the tool room where I would learn the basics of press tool design and come to understand the over-riding importance of this to the business. I was able to continue my studies at Aston Technical College, and in the evening I attended a business management course at South Birmingham Polytechnic, which proved to be most useful.

When compared with the highly organised business of AEI Birlec, working at Haden Bros. seemed to be chaotic to say the least. The systems in the office were practical, if a little old-fashioned, but in the factory there were no clearly defined areas of status or responsibility. Deciding what to make was left to the works manager in consultation with the stores foreman on a rather *ad hoc* basis, and stocks of raw materials, work in progress and finished goods were consequently very high. Somehow, it did work, but not in an efficient manner, and there were many unresolved arguments as to who was responsible when things went wrong.

The workforce was dominated by several families, often made up of two or three generations—a common arrangement in local industry at that time. The women would be power press operators or gas welders, the girls would operate hand presses, the boys would be drilling machine operators. The men would be labourers or tool setter-charge hands. Almost without exception, everyone who worked on the shop floor lived close by in mostly Victorian back-to-back houses, with shared outside toilets. They all walked to work. Later, as the slums were knocked down, that all changed and the majority came by bus from the new estates built on the east side of the city. We were fortunate to be close to good bus routes from those outer city housing areas.

In 1961 factory production was mainly that of bicycle frame components—frame lugs and fork crowns—which we supplied to cycle manufacturers in Birmingham and the Black Country where the majority of the industry was based. These parts would be assembled up by our customers into forks and frames—the initial steps in bicycle production. Apart from the plain tubes, there were, in fact, no parts of a bicycle frame and fork that we could not supply. Local customers at that time included such well-known names as Comrade, Dawes, Wearwell, Viking, Gundle, Pashley, Standard Cycles, Birmingham Bicycle (owned by Halfords), CWS, and Coventry Eagle.

Since the mid 1950s, my father had been keen to expand our range of cycle components, a policy which was to lead to a continuous process of development as the demand for different models continued. We had a particularly close working relationship with Gerry O'Donovan of Raleigh Special Products Division who was very helpful in suggesting new designs for frame lugs and fork crowns. At their factory in Worksop, new ideas on bicycle frame construction were being developed, and we later became

Haden frame components built into a Raleigh-Carlton cycle frame.

involved in some of their early work on the use of adhesives and hi-tech materials such as carbon fibre tube.

We also made large quantities of steel pressings and welded assemblies to customers' own designs, principally for Land Rover, but also for several other local manufacturers in the automotive industry. Although our particular

Miscellaneous Haden components.

speciality was cycle parts, we were in essence a typical Birmingham 'metal bashing' company—production methods centred around press work, welding and machining. In those days we employed about sixty people.

After twelve months of working in the factory, it became clear to me that there was an urgent need to introduce a formal production control system, and for all those who had a supervisory role to define their precise responsibilities. We were lucky in having some very experienced people working for us. My father agreed to give me a free hand to make changes: after clearly identifying different departments and who was in charge of each, defining everyone's roles, enhancing employment terms, and setting up a production control system that related more directly to customers' orders and schedules, we soon had a good team where everyone worked together, rather than in conflict with each other.

We were particularly fortunate in having an excellent machine shop foreman, Albert Collins, who with his very capable young tool setter Jack Danks, set an example of how things should and could be done. Sadly, Albert was soon to be taken seriously ill, but his shoes were quickly filled by Jack who, in his new position as foreman, was very good at getting the other foremen to work together, thus ensuring that there was a constant flow of finished goods being supplied on time into the stores. Members of the Danks family were to play an important role in the future development of the company.

Others who stood out were the reliable and loyal Ray Clarke in charge of inspection and packing, and Bill Mustin, foreman of our press shop. They did an excellent job, supported by a first rate team in the tool room, including the amazing Jack Chambers who had worked at our Princip Factory before the war and remembered my grandfather. If need be, he could make a set of press tools over the course of a weekend—a job that would normally take at least a week. I found Bill Douglas, the amiable works manager, easy to deal with, and we worked well together, introducing a proper management structure and keeping everyone happy.

An Opportunity to Expand

The early 1960s was an exciting time, for after many years of inexorable decline, there was a growing prosperity throughout the country. City institutions like the Stock Exchange and Lloyd's opened their boardrooms to those previously looked upon as 'the interfering middle classes'. In the new meritocracy, the sharpest minds showed how immoderate amounts of wealth could be obtained through takeover bids, asset stripping and property speculation. This was the period of mini cars and mini skirts, and in August 1962 we had our first contact with

Moulton bike, Design Centre Award winner, 1964.

a slightly eccentric, but extremely well-read, engineer with impressive business connections in the motor industry—Alex Moulton. Following the extraordinary success of the new Austin Mini car, he had the idea of producing a bicycle which also had small wheels and rubber suspension, and which he had cleverly designed so that it could easily be taken apart and stowed into the boot of a car.

The poet Philip Larkin famously wrote 'sexual intercourse began in nineteen-sixty-three, between the end of the Chatterley ban and the Beatles first LP.' So also began the Rolling Stones and production of the Moulton bicycle. In this invention was a ground-breaking concept that awoke a sleeping industry still locked to the tradition of established pre-war bicycle designs. Alex Moulton came to us on the recommendation of Raleigh, who saw us as a possible supplier of the many special parts required. The close business relationship which soon developed was to continue for many years.

Meanwhile, just a couple of months before I was about to celebrate my twenty-first birthday, we received a visit from one of the directors of J. A. Phillips Ltd., the large cycle and accessory manufacturer in Smethwick. They were in the process of merging with T. I. Raleigh in Nottingham and had decided to cease all production of cycle frame parts. We were asked if we would take over their outstanding order book and stocks of finished parts, which we were naturally very pleased to do. Bramptons, as their frame component manufacturing subsidiary was known, was in effect our major British competitor in this field, and we could see that this would provide a golden opportunity to not just increase our sales of bicycle parts, but also to improve profit margins. In order to help manage the huge intake of Bramptons' finished stock, we purchased a second-hand prefabricated bungalow and erected it on a piece of unused ground we owned at the rear of the factory. Bramptons had a wonderful sales slogan 'We don't make bicycles, we make them possible', and there was an expectation amongst independent bicycle manufacturers that we would take on this mantle.

Much of the business passed to us by Bramptons was in the form of export orders for Commonwealth countries. An example of this was in Australia where there were about twenty small manufacturers spread around the coast making only a few hundred cycles each year. The largest

Early Brampton advertisement by Cecil Aldin.

was Messrs General Accessories (Genacs) who insisted that all frame lugs had the shape of the Star of David cut into them. In total, we were exporting to thirty countries at around that time.

It was in those days that we first made contact with Philip Lieberman in Rhodesia. He was in the process of setting up a bicycle manufacturing plant in that country, having up until then been the importer and distributor for the Birmingham cycle manufacturer J. A. Phillips Ltd. We were asked to supply frame fittings, and although volumes were not large, this was to become regular business. We were pleased to be able to keep his company supplied with essential parts during the difficult period in the late 1970s when trade sanctions were applied prior to independence.

Later, in May 1980, I travelled to Rhodesia, now newly named Zimbabwe, and then on to South Africa, visiting several customers. Philip Lieberman's son Julian had taken over the management of their various family businesses following the death of his father, and for me to visit an African country in a state of turmoil as the politicians fought for control was not without its risks. I was somewhat alarmed on arrival when Julian told me that for safety reasons he had sent his family down to South Africa for a short period, but I was not to worry because he had a rifle and handgun ready in the house in case of any intruders during the night. Julian was a generous host, and I very much enjoyed my few days visiting his factory and staying in his large house in Bulawayo.

My introduction to an understanding of African politics actually came on the flight from London when I found that Robert Mugabe and I were the only two passengers in first class. Newly elected as Prime Minister, Mugabe was returning home after attending the funeral of Marshall Tito in Yugoslavia and I had several most interesting conversations with him. Shortly after the refuelling stop in Nairobi, where we were joined by other passengers, a young black man burst through into our cabin and prostrated himself on the floor in front of 'our great leader', saying words to the effect that he and his friends had killed three white farmers and raped two of their wives, and could he now be given two acres of land and a cow. He was rather unceremoniously picked up and dragged away, not to be seen again. When we landed in Harare I accompanied Mugabe down the steps to the red carpet, to be greeted by various officials and diplomats, a never-to-be-forgotten troupe of well-endowed dancing girls in traditional costumes, and a huge cheering crowd.

While in South Africa, I had the opportunity of visiting the large Raleigh factory on the outskirts of Johannesburg and met their managing director, Kevin O'Donovan. Like me he had been brought up in Sutton Coldfield, the affluent residential town favoured by the families of many of the cycle and cycle component manufacturers who had factories in Birmingham. The O'Donovan family were originally owners of Carlton Cycles, a company which became part of Raleigh in 1960.

Alex Moulton

The close working relationship that we formed with Alex Moulton and his team of engineers in the 1960s was to prove mutually beneficial. Initially, he had asked Raleigh to manufacture his special small wheel bicycle, but they could see that first it would require a great deal of re-engineering and would not fit easily into their established production facilities. Therefore they declined to be involved.

Alex decided to go ahead with manufacture on his own and I well remember the day that he first called to see us. After leaving his Rolls-Royce at the British Motor Corporation (BMC) factory in Longbridge on the south side of Birmingham, where he had important business connections, he cycled to visit Reynolds Tube Co. in Tyseley (east Birmingham) and then came on to us. Arriving at our offices in Westley Street with a large bundle of drawings, he left his prototype bicycle out in the street leaning against the office wall, with no apparent conception that Birmingham was a rather different sort of place to his home town of Bradford-on-Avon in Wiltshire. My father persuaded him that perhaps it would be a good idea to bring it into the reception area. The meeting proved to be very constructive. Alex was anxious to build a few prototype bicycles to put on display in the November 1962 Cycle Exhibition at Earls Court, London.

A few days later, he placed orders with us to tool up for the production of the many special parts, with a particular request for twenty sets to be fabricated by hand if necessary in order to meet the show deadline. Our tool room worked many long hours to achieve this. I remember the satisfaction of visiting Earls Court with my father, where Alex was particularly generous in his praise for the substantial contribution we had made, without which he would not have been able to exhibit that year.

The reception at the show was overwhelming and Alex realised that the factory he was building in the grounds of his family estate outside Bradford-on-Avon would not be large enough to meet demand. By good fortune, the directors of BMC were keen to become involved. Alex was a close friend of Alec (later Sir) Issigonis and knew the directors well through his developmental work on motor vehicle rubber suspension units.

And so it was that through BMC's subsidiary, Fisher and Ludlow, a production assembly line was set up in July 1963 at the new Fisher Bendix washing machine factory at Kirkby, near Liverpool. Here they were soon to produce six hundred bicycles per week. Almost without exception, the members of the workforce were strong supporters of Liverpool Football Club and during the season, if Liverpool had an evening home match, it could be almost guaranteed that a mechanical fault would occur in the assembly line during the late afternoon. As a result the shift workers had to be laid off until the following morning whilst repairs were carried out.

Meanwhile, Alex's staff back home were producing two to three hundred bicycles per week in their purpose-built factory alongside the River Avon. Large orders were placed with us to supply a multitude of parts to both factories, including complete front and rear fork assemblies, as well as a very complex internal steering column, inside which the front suspension unit fitted. We supplied about thirty different parts for each bicycle, which meant that at the peak of demand we were supplying twenty-seven thousand parts per week in individual or sub-assembly form.

As a result of these contracts we developed a close working relationship with Tube Products Ltd. in Oldbury. Like us, they were specialists in all forms of tube manipulation and were a principal supplier of frame tubes and special parts to Moultons, as well as to the rest of the UK cycle industry.

From the profits generated as a result of business with Moultons, we were able, in 1965, to move our offices to an extended upper floor where we could incorporate better design and drawing office facilities. The lower ground floor offices were converted into a modern tool room well equipped for the development of new products. As time progressed, we were able to invest in new manufacturing plant and replace much of the pre-war machinery, some of which had belonged to my grandfather.

Fifty thousand of a simpler, 14-inch-wheel children's version of the Moulton bicycle—the Moulton Junior 1970—were manufactured under licence by Triang Toys in their Birmingham factory, incorporating many parts supplied by ourselves. That factory, which had originally been the Unique and Unity Bicycle Co., was acquired by Raleigh after the demise of Triang's owner (Lines Brothers) in 1971.

Alex also designed another 14-inch-wheel model, the Mini, which was more suitable in size for ladies, smaller adults and teenage children. It was scaled to roughly seven-eighths of a full-size Moulton.

Despite the innovative brilliance of Moulton's original idea, it soon became clear that improvements were necessary to strengthen the bicycle's rear end. Because of the suspension arrangements there, the chain stays were not supported by seat stays connected to the seat tube in the normal manner, and the rear wheel was not, therefore, always maintained in a vertical position. Alex's unrelenting desire to achieve weight reduction, and the consequent failure to provide sufficient strength within the design to withstand bicycle mishandling, meant that several other engineering changes were necessary. These included the need to strengthen the unsupported rear carrier and to improve the front suspension arrangement. In addition to all this, there was an ongoing plan to look at possible design changes that might reduce manufacturing costs.

The almost continuous introduction of modifications caused considerable irritation at Fisher and Ludlow. They had complex procedures to follow, based on motor industry standards, and their systems could not cope with the rapid introduction of all the changes that Alex wanted. As a result, it was agreed that unless really essential, changes would be delayed and only introduced as a complete package every few months.

And so it was not long before Alex involved us closely in the development of the more robust Series 2 models. I remember many enthralling days spent at Bradford-on-Avon exploring new ideas with his chief engineer, Phil Uncles, with whom we developed a particularly good working relationship. Alex was a generous host, and to be invited to join him for lunch in his magnificent Jacobean mansion was always an enjoyable occasion, the only problem being his intensity. His extraordinary way of questioning and analysing in detail everything that was spoken about could leave you feeling quite exhausted afterwards. In forty-three years of business he was the only customer I can recall who said from the start that he expected our prices to contain a minimum profit margin of ten per cent.

It was not long before other bicycle manufacturers entered the market, having sensed the latent demand for 'something new' foreseen by Alex Moulton. Raleigh produced the RSW16 small wheeler. This was a bicycle with small, heavy, fat tyres rather than suspension, but was well-engineered and carried the Raleigh name. With subsequent improvements, being marketed at a realistic trade price and supported by enormous publicity, there is no doubt that it severely damaged Moulton's position in the market.

With a reduction in demand and mounting losses, production of Moulton bicycles ceased in 1967. Alex sold out to Raleigh and entered into a consultancy arrangement, the result of which was a Mark 3 model,

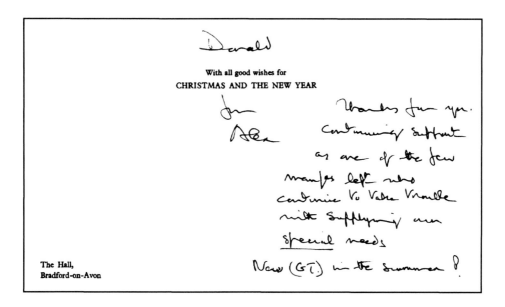

Alex Moulton in front of The Hall with his early range of bicycles

the simpler design being heavily influenced by the Raleigh drawing office. This new model was made in Nottingham without any Haden parts. The design was not liked by Alex and did not sell well. Only five thousand were manufactured. In 1975 Raleigh agreed to end the consultancy so that Alex could develop his own separate ideas back at Bradford-on-Avon, with a view to small-scale production there of more sophisticated models.

One of the legacies of the battle between Moulton and Raleigh was the realisation that there was a market for a new type of lady's shopping cycle. This was quickly taken up by Comrade Cycle, Dawes and Halmanco (Halfords cycle factory in Wales) with excellent hybrid designs built using 18-inch or 20-inch diameter wheels and an open frame. This was an opportunity for us to make special lugs and other new frame components, the demand from Comrade Cycles in Darlaston being particularly strong.

Alex went on to design a more up-market machine where the cost of production was not so critical. His new frame was made of a multitude of small diameter tubes, influenced no doubt in part by the famous nineteenth-century Dursley Pedersen. This new design represented in every respect an improvement over his previous models, and I remember him telling me that he wanted his new bicycles to have the same technical and quality image as that of a Jaguar car. We were asked to supply several special components and had a continuing relationship with his small production unit in Bradford-on-Avon for many years. We also supplied parts for his more economically priced APB model, manufactured under licence by Pashley Cycles in Stratford-upon-Avon.

In 2009, Alex published a monumental autobiography detailing his extraordinary achievements in the aircraft, automobile and bicycle industries, a fascinating book that should be compulsory reading for any student of engineering. I found it rather disappointing, therefore, that he omitted to mention anywhere, the enormous contribution that I know we made, and which he privately acknowledged many times in our conversations. Indeed, he told me that he considered it essential that I should write my own book to enable others to understand a little of what he saw as the important contribution we had made to the bicycle and motorcycle industry over many years.

A Changing Market for Bicycles

The merger in 1962 of Phillips and Raleigh created an unbalanced home market. In earlier years, Raleigh had already absorbed two of their major competitors, BSA and Hercules, and so were now in an even more dominant position, with about 60 per cent of the home market. This left the remaining manufacturers competing against each other for a reduced segment, as by 1973 the whole industry was facing a rising tide of imports. The manufacturing capacity of the independent manufactures, based mainly in Birmingham and the Black Country, was at that time about eight thousand bicycles per week, of whom Comrade was the largest. Excluding Raleigh, there were in all about twenty UK bicycle manufacturers, mostly small, rather old-fashioned family businesses headed by a pre-war generation, making traditional models. Many were soon to fall by the wayside.

Increased disposable income and the availability of cheap family cars meant that the working classes no longer saw the bicycle as a prime means of transport, and while the Moulton phenomenon and its derivatives had provided some welcome relief, cycles were no longer seen as the first choice of Christmas present for teenagers. At the same time, the independent component manufacturers found it increasingly difficult to survive as their home market reduced and many were soon to go out of business. There were some new opportunities here for Hadens; we were in a position to take over the tooling and production of several discontinued lines, including some parts previously made by Bayliss Wiley and Co. Ltd.

There was, however, a respite when an increased demand for sports bicycles emerged in the early 1970s, driven by the American keep-fit craze. The subsequent increase in orders for our traditional products gave us ten years of profitable growth at a time when the engineering industry in Birmingham was going into rapid decline. It has been said that in the ten year period from 1971, two hundred thousand manufacturing jobs were lost in Birmingham alone.[1]

In the 1970s, as part of a strategy to reduce the influence of the Republican movement in Northern Ireland, the British government was

---

1. Dr Steven McCabe, Birmingham Business School.

pumping almost indecent amounts of money into the regional economy and looking for opportunities to introduce new manufacturing jobs. The Northern Ireland Development Corporation (NIDC) decided that a bicycle factory in Derry might work. Frank Clements, a well-known ex-racing cyclist who represented a number of overseas component suppliers, gave advice and the new company was soon established using the brand name of Viking Cycles. Seeing an opportunity, Richard Cross of TD Cross and Sons Ltd. (manufacturers of head and bottom bracket fittings), Eric Healey of Blumel Bros. Ltd. (mudguard manufacturers), and I decided to pay them a visit. Having flown to Belfast, we hired a five-seater aircraft together with pilot and co-pilot and flew to Derry, landing in a grass field known locally as Derry International Airport. After a very liquid lunch, we came away with promises of orders and flew on to Dublin for a dinner we had arranged for Irish bicycle wholesalers.

In order to promote the new business of Viking Cycles, the NIDC decided to approach a well-known television star who was also an ex-racing cyclist. His name was Jimmy Saville. At that time, of course, his later-to-be-revealed criminal behaviour was not public knowledge. There is a story that having been informed that the new project was backed by the Government, Saville said his price for helping would be a knighthood. This was indeed awarded to him a few years later, although the suggestion that this might be connected to the promotional work he did for Viking Cycles in Londonderry could never be proven.

Canada Cycle and Motor Co. (CCM)

We had a long-standing customer in Toronto, Canada, known by their brand name as CCM, who traditionally made cycles in the summer and hockey skates in the winter. The American keep-fit craze that began in the 1970s soon spread to Canada, and in order to take advantage of the huge increase in demand for bicycles, they expanded their production from about one thousand to six thousand units per week. Purchase orders for cycle frame lug sets, fork crowns and bottom bracket shells were placed with us accordingly. With our own capacity limited to about twelve thousand sets per week, we were now under considerable pressure in the factory, but we had an excellent team who were ready to rise to the occasion. We were able to negotiate with CCM very rewarding prices, generating healthy profits that we reinvested in a new factory extension and some improved manufacturing methods.

In the course of our dealings with CCM, I got to know their manufacturing vice president Ces Matthews very well. He would often call in to see us while visiting his European suppliers and I would visit their factory on a regular basis. One night, whilst being entertained for dinner in his apartment in Toronto, he told me a story about being stationed in Weston-super-Mare just after the war. He was part of a Canadian army engineering unit which had been given the task of dismantling the coastal defence guns on the Brean Down headland. He remembered that every day, to get onto the track to the headland, they had to pass in their large army lorry through a farm yard, and would throw sweets to two little boys who rushed out of the house to open the gate. This is an extraordinary coincidence, since I am sure the two little boys he referred to were my brother and I, then only about four years old. We used to spend our summer holidays on the farm owned by the Bowley family and enjoyed, as all young boys do, seeing the soldiers and their army vehicles pass by. We also enjoyed wonderful fresh country food, while those back home were still having to survive on wartime rations.

The author (*left*) with his brother Peter, hunting in Gloucestershire, 1986.

EXPORT AWARD FOR SMALLER MANUFACTURERS 1973/74

THIS IS TO CERTIFY THAT

Haden Bros. Limited

ARE WINNERS OF THE

EXPORT AWARD FOR SMALLER MANUFACTURERS 1973/74

PANEL OF JUDGES

Lord Feather, CBE

R. M. Hilary, MBE, TD,
Deputy Chairman and Commercial
Director, British Airways BOAC

P. de Laszlo,
President,
Smaller Businesses Association

J. A. Raven,
Director General,
Association of British Chambers
of Commerce

J. S. Rooke, CMG, OBE,
Chief Executive,
British Overseas Trade Board

Nicolas Tate,
Regional & Smaller Firms Director,
Confederation of British Industry

DATE *14th March, 1974.*

In 1974 we received a special export award in the form of an engraved glass goblet, an award which we won largely thanks to our substantial exports to Canada. This was presented to us at a special ceremony in London by the Association of British Chambers of Commerce, sponsored by British Airways and the CBI. My father went to receive this because I was in hospital with a slipped disc. I had fallen badly from my horse while out fox hunting—a sport I had only just then taken up, and which has since provided me with a lifetime of fun and many very good friends.

New Products

In 1976 we carried out a comprehensive review of our range of cycle components and identified a need to add additional products to meet changing market demands. We introduced new frame lug designs, and some new steel bottom bracket shells initially obtained from Japan. Our research particularly highlighted a market for precision investment cast cycle fork crowns. Our first new model, made by what is known as the lost wax process, was designed by us for use on only the world's most expensive bicycles. Rolls-Royce, experts in this manufacturing process through their production of aircraft turbine blades, agreed to produce for us the special castings which we subsequently machined. It was fascinating to see our parts coming off the same production line as the iconic Spirit of Ecstasy statuette that has appeared on the radiator of every Rolls-Royce motor car since 1911.

Japanese Technology

In 1978 we acquired an additional factory in nearby Bolton Street where we installed high-tech hydraulic bulge forming machinery, enabling us to manufacture cycle bottom bracket shells from steel tube. The need for this change of manufacturing process arose from the difficulty of obtaining malleable white heart castings, traditionally made for us in the Black Country. We would buy these castings in and machine them to accurate sizes ready for cycle frame assembly

Haden No. 2 factory, Bolton Street.

and brazing. The decline of heavy industry in that area in the late 1960s had led to the closure of many foundries and we decided that we should look at a different means of production.

My father was initially keen that we should consider making bottom bracket shells from flat steel, a rather labour intensive process. After some experimentation we decided not to proceed down that route, but instead, and after considerable investigation, negotiated a contract with a Japanese company Eisho Seisakusho Co. Ltd. in Osaka. This was an agreement to purchase not just the machines, but also all the tooling made to their patented designs to enable us to now make bottom bracket shells from steel tube. As part of the arrangement, we sent two of our works staff to Eisho's factory for ten days so that they could study the manufacturing process and learn how to operate the machinery. Over a period of time, we formed a close working relationship with their managing director, Tatami Akamatsu, and they purchased some of our top-of-the-range cycle parts for sale in Japan.

Eisho were the prime manufacturer in Japan of cycle frame lugs and bottom bracket shells, and so we had a lot in common. Visits to their factory were always of great interest and we were allowed to freely photograph all of their processes. Their business was very similar to ours, being a primarily father and son managed operation, and visits both ways were always most constructive and enjoyable. I was particularly struck by the reverence they had for British culture and our industrial history. They loved to go gambling, and I shall never forget the look of huge awe and respect on Tatami Akamatsu's face in April 1982 as we sat, one night, in a Birmingham casino watching on television the two aircraft carriers HMS *Hermes* and HMS *Invincible* departing from Portsmouth to engage in the Falklands conflict. He was so taken by what he saw that he stood up and, as a huge gesture of respect, bowed very low first to me and then to the television set.

Press shop, Bolton Street factory.

Two-hundred-tonne hydraulic bulge forming press for the production of bicycle bottom bracket shells.

Like us, they were later to be very badly affected by the great worldwide reduction in demand for traditional cycle frame components.

Dixon Vaughan Ltd.

In 1982 we were approached by Steve Hodgson, the owner of Messrs Dixon Vaughan Ltd., a local company in nearby Lombard Street. That company was first established in 1838 as a manufacturer of cast iron parts for horse drawn carriages. Later, they made cycle frame components, specialising in parts for heavy-duty tradesman bicycles, and they had a valuable ongoing contract for the supply of parts for Post Office carrier bikes. We reached an agreement that we would purchase all Dixon Vaughan's machinery and tooling and move it to our Westley Street factory. Our machine shop foreman, Jack Danks, did an excellent job absorbing all this into his department—he was a tower of strength in everything he did.

These new products proved at that time to be a useful addition to our range, as they were of high value even though volumes were relatively small. Steve Hodgson joined us as export sales manager, but I declined to take on any of his employees, some of whom had worked for us previously. They were of Pakistani origin, had a different set of values, demanded special extra holidays, spoke very little English, and had, at one time, ganged up on us insisting on a wage increase with the threat that otherwise they would leave; which they did.

Subsequently, I was pleased to have an understanding with our shop steward, Ray Moore, that there would be no objection to us taking 'country of origin' into account during the engagement process. This was a time of increasing unemployment and there was a strong feeling amongst our workforce that available jobs should not go to foreign workers. We had a clear understanding on this matter with our local Labour Exchange who, off the record, agreed not to send newly arrived immigrants for interviews that would be quite pointless. This saved time being wasted on all sides.

The Sinclair C5 Electric Tricycle, 1984–85

I am glad we were never involved in this crazy project. It was perhaps the most extreme example of an ill-thought out business venture, a silly idea pushed forward by an eccentric inventor with money to throw away. I could never understand how anyone could think that, in 1985,

Sinclair electric tricycle.

people would want to pay £399 for a battery-powered assisted tricycle with a very limited range, where the rider sat at bumper height relative to other vehicles, with the prospect of looking up underneath lorry wheel arches. To add insult to injury, rear view mirrors and a few other essential extras were offered for an additional £143.

With the help of Government grants, production facilities were developed at the Hoover factory in South Wales, based on estimated sales of four thousand units per week. The vehicle was launched on 10 January 1985 and proved to be a complete disaster, even though some three million pounds had been spent on an advertising campaign. On 12 October that year, the business was placed in the hands of the receiver and entered voluntary liquidation in November. The total losses on the project were estimated at more than £10 million.

BMX and Mountain Bikes

The American craze for sports bikes that had started in the early 1970s had spread to other developed countries, and it soon became clear that the traditional European component industry could not cope with the demand for parts. As a result, new component manufacturers began to emerge in the Far East, and with the improvements in welding technology, new cycle frame designs began to appear with larger diameter tubes made from more exotic materials. At first the craze was for teenage motocross-type bikes known as BMX, and we introduced a set of frame and fork parts enabling these to be built using traditional manufacturing methods.

It was not long before a new type of adult cycle appeared, robust enough to ride at speed down mountain tracks, of which there are an abundance in the USA. These new machines had straight handlebars, front fork suspension and a wide range of gears and were, therefore, by coincidence, more suitable for urban riding than the traditional drop handlebar sports cycle which they were soon to replace.

By 1987 the 'mountain' bike had become, and has remained, the dominant model type with similar, but less exotic, machines made for day-to-day use. The principal feature that now began to affect Hadens was the severe reduction in demand for traditional frame components, for not only were bicycle frames increasingly being welded without frame fittings, but by this time the number of good quality, cheap bicycles being

Cycle Spanners   # HADEN

TD CROSS MIO/BROOKS No. 3
PEG AND CONE SPANNER.

TD CROSS M11/BROOKS No. 7
COMBINATION 6 WAY SPANNER

TD CROSS M12
TENSION SPANNER.

TD CROSS M13/BROOKS No. 8
COMBINATION 4 WAY SPANNER.

TD CROSS M14/BROOKS No. 6
HEAD AND LOCK RING SPANNER.

All components supplied with zinc plated finish unless otherwise requested.

Exclusively manufactured by

HADEN BROS. LIMITED

WESTLEY STREET, BIRMINGHAM B9 4ES. ENGLAND.
TELEPHONE: 021-772 0461.   TELEX 334248   HADEN G.   KB 183

imported was slowly destroying the UK bicycle manufacturing industry. Between 1978 and 1986, the largest manufacturer, Raleigh, saw annual sales fall from two million to one million units. The whole of the UK bicycle manufacturing sector was in rapid decline and for us, the era of bulk production of frame parts was coming to an end. Within the bicycle industry, we had to rely increasingly on supplying bespoke parts for niche sections of the market.

Bicycle Accessories

Since the early 1950s we had made a range of cycle front forks including a chrome plated 27-inch sports replacement. We also made an extensive range of steel handlebar stems. My father was a clever engineer and owned several patents which he had taken out in the 1950s relating to the design of these. We also supplied separate parts to other companies who made their own stems. Demand for steel handlebar stems fell off in the mid 1960s as cheap alloy types became available from France and Italy. We ceased production of stems around 1975, being more preoccupied with the increased demand at that time for frame components.

By 1980 many of the UK bicycle component manufacturers were facing a difficult time because of the huge influx of cheap, but well made, components from the Far East. As many of these companies closed down, some new opportunities arose for us and we were delighted with the arrangements made in 1983 to take on the production of some accessory items such as cycle spanners, lamp brackets and seat pillars following the unfortunate closure of T. D. Cross and Sons and the J. A. Phillips component factory in Smethwick. These two companies kindly passed on to us their press tools, and subsequently we were able to manufacture and sell up to thirty thousand combination six-way spanners (TD Cross M11 and Brooks no. 7) per month in the spring and summer seasons, mostly through Halfords stores.

We also supplied large numbers of gear protectors to Raleigh in Nottingham. This

New cycle accessories and tools introduced at IFMA, Cologne, 1984.

was a device mounted onto the axle of a mountain bike to protect the derailleur gear. The part we made was to their own design, but we additionally made our own different models for sale in the aftermarket.

The Bicycle Association of Great Britain

This is the trade association of the bicycle industry based in Coventry, membership originally being limited to UK manufacturers of bicycles and bicycle parts. We had been a member in the immediate post-war period, but this had lapsed, and in 1977 I persuaded my father that we should rejoin because this would give us a discount when participating in UK trade shows and considerable assistance when exhibiting overseas.

For several years we took part in the New York International Cycle Show. There was always a good relationship between the British exhibitors and we would usually try to stay at the same hotel and spend the evenings together. At that time, we were particularly close to TI Reynolds, manufacturers of the then famous 531 tubing. We shared many customers, as Reynolds tubes fitted Haden lugs.

Tom Field, their sales manager, had a friend in New York who was an undercover policeman, and one night he took us out in his battered old car to an Italian restaurant in a rather shady part of town. I remember feeling rather alarmed when I saw the bullet holes in the side of the car. Later he took us on a late night tour of the NYPD Fifth Avenue Precinct (Police) Station—it was just like watching a scene out of an American gangster movie.

The New York Cycle Show was always in the last week of February, and it was a great bonus to be able to travel home via Bermuda, Barbados or Antigua and enjoy a week or so of sunshine while still on business expenses.

We also participated in the bi-annual International Cycle and Motorcycle Show in Cologne, West Germany, at that time the largest cycle and motorcycle show in the world. This was hard work, but always great fun. We were well-known for putting on a 'beer and sandwich' party on the first night at a local hotel, to which we invited not just our customers, but also other British exhibitors, as well as our main competitors. This major exhibition was a great opportunity for our

HADEN MAKE IT 125 YEARS!
Cologne supper celebration

There is very good reason to congratulate any business that makes it past the Centenary and when you get to add another 25 years then a bottle or two should pop. History points to the Haden operation in Birmingham being the oldest bicycle components supplier in the business, another good reason to celebrate.

In Cologne during IFMA Donald Haden – boasting a badge which said 'I'm 125' hosted a party that continued their tradition of an evening social and jolly – and here (*second right*) he is pictured with (*left to right*) Nick Sanders, Sturmey Archer; Richard Cross, Dillglove; and Stewart Tibbatts, Reynolds 531 Ltd

Above, article from *Bicycle Trade and Industry*, September 1994. (reprinted with thanks to Peter Lumley).

Right, Scott and John Danks on the cross channel ferry travelling to the IFMA cycle and motorcycle show in Cologne, 1994.

Below, NEC, Birmingham, 1981.

senior staff to meet many others in the industry and enjoy a little of life beyond the end of the telephone.

Other overseas bicycle shows we took part in were in Barcelona and Paris. We also exhibited at cycle shows in London (Olympia), at Harrogate and at the NEC in Birmingham.

Re-joining the Bicycle Association gave me the opportunity, through being on various committees, to get to know a lot of people I had not previously had the opportunity to meet, including most of the directors of Raleigh. In 1982 I was elected for a five-year term as chairman of the accessory and component manufacturers group, taking over from my great friend John Cross of T. D. Cross and Sons Ltd. That company made cycle headsets, axle sets, freewheels and sprockets, and we knew them well, both families having had close connections over several generations.

As part of my duties I was expected to attend lunches in the House of Commons, lobbying for the interests of the cycle industry, meeting government ministers and others. The Bicycle Association was pleased to have the support of a group of MPs known as the All Party Friends of Cycling. Their chairman was the influential Jack Dormand who had excellent connections through his position as chairman of the Parliamentary Labour Party. They were represented in the House of Lords by Lord Craigavon, whose grandfather had been the first prime minister of Northern Ireland.

At least once a year, by arrangement with one of our MP supporters, the Bicycle Association would hire a private dining room in the House of Commons and have an enjoyable lunch with a cross section of members from both Houses. I remember one particular lunch sitting next to John Prescott, who at that time was shadow minister of transport, later to be deputy prime minister. I worry even now at the thought that this man was once left in charge of the country when prime minister Tony Blair was abroad. I came to the conclusion that he was possibly one of the most obnoxious people I had ever met. On another occasion I remember a hilarious evening in the House of Lords dining room as a guest of the delightful Lord Craigavon—there were just six of us sitting down, including Gerry Fitt and Ian Paisley. In the summer we would usually host a drinks party on the House of Commons terrace, directly overlooking the River Thames—an opportunity to meet a large cross section of MPs and peers.

At that time I used to travel to Brussels twice a year, representing the UK industry at meetings of European bicycle and bicycle parts manufacturers, where matters supposedly of common interest were discussed. At these meetings I rather innocently expected delegates to be divided roughly between those from the north of the EEC and those from the south. The reality turned out to be Germany versus the rest of Europe. I am pleased to record that, thanks to our efforts, and unlike in international football, the Germans did not always win.

It was certainly most interesting to experience at first hand the process by which the EEC appeared to work—consultants producing glossy brochures for other consultants to read, vast concrete office blocks in sea-green and bronze where Eurocrats drawing huge salaries no doubt spent their days laughing cynically over this new world of directives. The streets always seemed to be full of chauffeur-driven cars and taxis presumably taking people from meeting to meeting. And who paid for all this, and was any of it really necessary? The restaurants certainly did well.

On one occasion, we invited our European friends to London and had a grand dinner by special invitation at the Cavalry and Guards Club in Piccadilly. That night I returned late to the Berkeley Hotel to find a note under my bedroom door addressed to the Argentine ambassador asking him to most urgently telephone his office at the United Nations, New York. The request to telephone was underlined three times, but having enjoyed an excellent dinner I rather irresponsibly threw the note in the bin. The next day Argentine forces invaded the Falklands.

The Centenary Club

In 1939 leading figures in the bicycle industry formed their own cycling club, celebrating the centenary of what is believed by many to be the invention of the bicycle by the Scotsman Kirkpatrick Macmillan at his blacksmith's forge in Dumfriesshire. Over a period of several years, it was suggested by friends that I might join the club, but I had always declined, feeling that Monday to Friday each week was enough engagement with the industry. However, in 1979, at the invitation of Dick Pashley, I agreed to go along for a weekend based in Ross-on-Wye, not far from home.

Richard Dawes kindly lent me a bike and I thoroughly enjoyed myself. It was not long before I was invited to join the committee and in May 1991 I took over as club secretary for five years, organising a total of ten weekend runs, including one in Holland and one in France.

The cycling is not too serious and is predominantly designed to cater for those who would never otherwise get in the saddle. I expect I shall be remembered as the secretary who introduced the idea of two pub stops before lunch instead of one. For my efforts, the members kindly invited me in 1997 to become president. The club has an annual black tie dinner and we usually manage to have an interesting speaker.

Since leaving the industry I have, as a past president, been able to continue my club membership and attendance at committee meetings. This has been a much appreciated opportunity to keep in touch with old friends.

Engineering Contracts

My father quite rightly had always seen the need to expand away from the cycle industry and our success in this was exemplified by the sub-contract work we did manufacturing pressings and welded assemblies, in particular for the Land Rover Company.

We supplied about twenty different parts to them, and in the 1980s this accounted for a substantial part of our turnover. It proved to be a great loss therefore in 1993 when, as part of a programme to substantially reduce their number of suppliers, they resourced elsewhere. In a subsequent meeting with their purchasing director, I felt obliged to disclose details of my observations which indicated a degree of corruption at that time in

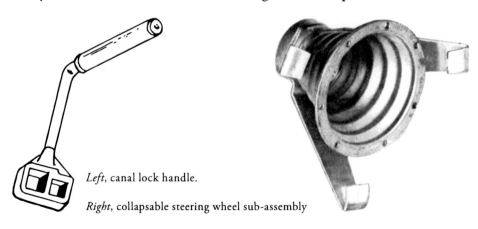

Left, canal lock handle.

Right, collapsable steering wheel sub-assembly

their buying office, although I was not able to link this with their decision to close our account.

In the early 1960s we supplied large numbers of television legs to Pye Ltd. in different sizes, and made a range of parts for stillages and steel pallets. Later we made canal lock handles for which there was a regular seasonal market replacing those lost overboard. Following new car safety design requirements in the 1970s, we manufactured collapsible steering wheel assemblies for Clifford Covering Co. These were for sale in the auto-parts aftermarket. We also made large numbers of transformer brackets and housings for portable welders and refrigerated container lorries.

In 1978 we took on a useful contract to make parts for Norlett, the Scandinavian manufacturer of garden equipment. They had designed a small garden cultivator, and initially came to us looking for a steel clamp similar to a lady's bicycle seat lug. When they saw the capacity we had for steel pressings and welded assemblies, they asked us to make all the cultivator's chassis parts, and we set up a special department to do this work in our Bolton street factory. This contract lasted several years and was very profitable.

Another contract about that time was for the supply of pressed steel assemblies that were part of a chain conveyor system for use in the mining industry in Australia. We supplied these for many years. The assembly consisted of two precision-made steel pressings welded together, for which we had to install heavy-duty projection welding machines. These machines were so powerful that they caused the lights to dim in nearby houses and we had no alternative but to install our own electricity sub-station.

For many years we supplied parts to Concentric Engineering Ltd., a major Birmingham manufacturer of automobile vehicle water pumps. We made the pressed steel top covers and other parts. This was good regular business in useful quantities.

In 1985 we entered into a major contract with Messrs Tickford Ltd., who were suppliers to the motor industry of specialist parts with a deserved reputation for product design and development. A sister company to Aston Martin at that time, Tickfords had a contract to design and supply the complete hood assembly for a new small Lotus sports car model (Elan M100). They were looking for a company who could tool up, manufacture and supply the many complex internal linkage parts required to support

Lotus Elan M100

and act as a mechanism to raise and lower the hood fabric. We enjoyed a good working relationship with Tickfords, and it was particularly rewarding to be involved not just in manufacturing, but also at the design stage. Their chief project engineer, who had previously held a similar position at Aston Martin, said how much he appreciated the valuable contribution we had made. For each hood assembly we supplied twenty parts, mostly made from round edge steel bar, some in extremely complex shapes. Apart from the initial presswork, parts were machined (holes drilled, etc.), welded and subsequently sent out for sub-contract painting.

We set up a special department to handle this work, and although the contract ran well for several years, we were disappointed that sales never reached the expected level. This was because the car had a serious rival in the very successful Mazda MX5. In total only 4,655 Elan cars were produced before production was moved to KIA (South Korea) who then made all their own parts.

Lotus were not known at that time for high manufacturing quality and one of the problems we were involved in trying to sort out arose because it was found that the overall width of vehicle body shells coming down their assembly line could vary by as much as two inches. This made a satisfactory fit of the hood assembly often impossible and there was therefore an ongoing problem with water leaking into the passenger compartment during inclement weather.

Tickfords was a very interesting company to deal with, employing some very competent engineers. They provided a valuable service to the motor manufacturers. One day, while I was in their factory I asked what they were doing stripping down brand new engines for a well-known Coventry car manufacturer. I was told that the car manufacturer had a serious engine design problem, and on a temporary basis, in order to keep production going, the engines had to be modified after they had been built. This was all done by Tickfords in great secrecy so as to preserve the manufacturer's good name, and all the windows in their factory had to be blacked out. Engines were delivered and collected only during the night so that no one in the industry or press would know what was going on.

We also manufactured parts for Austin and Morris Minis, the Ford Granada, TVR sports cars and David Brown tractors. There were many other parts we made for different companies in different industries, but the longest running contract we had was for the supply of large steel pressings for lorry air brakes. This business originated in the late 1960s when we received an enquiry from an American-owned company in Glasgow— Messrs Berg Ltd. That company was to change hands several times over the years, eventually moving to Redditch as Haldex Brake Products Ltd., still American-owned. We tooled up for several 'non pressure housings', as these parts were known. We also made some of the clamping bands that joined the caps to the main body. This all became very substantial business with large consignments leaving our factory several times every week. In the early days we had to buy large heavy-duty power presses as we found that the work was beyond the capacity of our standard equipment, and we installed special automated machines to weld threaded bosses to the side and top of each pressing. In 1985 we had the opportunity to purchase the neighbouring factory in Watery Lane and set up there a special self-contained department for the production of these parts. Over a period of more than thirty years, we manufactured many hundreds of thousands of these parts, accounting for about twenty-five per cent of our turnover.

The Final Years

Even though every effort was made to cut costs, the loss of the Land Rover contract in 1993, coupled with the reducing demand for our cycle products, soon brought down profits, and by 1997 we started to incur trading losses. Within the cycle trade, we still had good business with Pashley in Stratford-upon-Avon, who manufacture an outstanding range of special bicycles. Also we were pleased to be associated with the growing Brompton cycle factory in London, who produce an amazing folding bicycle for the commuting public. But the other UK manufacturers had all but ceased by now, or else reinvented themselves as importers of bicycles in complete or kit form.

All our staff worked extremely hard to ensure customers' requirements

Haden sales brochure, 1997

were met, but the underlying problem was that we had not been able to generate enough new business to replace that which had been lost, and year on year gross profit margins were reducing. It was now necessary to make savage cuts in our overheads and reduce the number of people we employed. We let out part of the factory to a tenant, who unfortunately proved to be almost more trouble than he was worth.

By this time, customers were increasingly finding themselves in a buyers' market. Closures in other Birmingham industries meant that a lot of presswork companies had surplus capacity, so buyers could demand price reductions every year, even though the cost of raw materials was going up. Another factor was the widespread increase in the use of plastics in place of steel. Many 'metal bashing' companies similar to ourselves in the West Midlands were in the same difficult position.

Life was not without its lighter moments. Driving to the office early one summer morning, I was somewhat surprised and amused to hear the news on the local radio station BRMB that a parrot had been seen flying into our factory and no one knew whose it was. It actually turned out to be an African grey and every morning for about a week the story was a humorous feature on the radio station, with telephone requests to our office for a regular update on the situation. Having spent several days and nights roosting in the rafters of our No. 2 press shop, the bird was eventually captured and taken home by one of our employees.

As we moved into 2002, it was became increasingly clear that we were faced with an impossible task in honestly preparing a budget that would show at least a break even position. Ironically, at this time we probably had the best management team that the company had ever had, but we were being buffeted and overwhelmed by powerful economic forces that were beyond our control. In May 2002, therefore, I came to the conclusion that as soon as we had completed existing orders, we would cease all production, liquidate stocks, and in an orderly manner arrange for all future production to be transferred to other sources.

We finally ceased production on 2 June 2002, a very difficult day, and I felt particularly sorry for those staff who had so loyally supported us to the end and had uncertain futures in front of them. However, it has been of some consolation to hear people say on many occasions since then that working at Hadens was the best job they ever had 'because it was always such fun'.

It would therefore be wrong to end this chapter without mentioning, for the record, the exemplary contribution of certain members of staff. My father's secretary, Sybil Ballinger, with her wide experience was always a great help in the office, and was particularly good with customers on the phone. John Melia, and subsequently Terry Mould, were hard working and very reliable as accounts managers. My secretary, Tina Hateley, who joined us in April 1974 had particular attributes which later enabled her to get a top secretarial job at Land Rover. There she demonstrated her special capabilities in a number of different positions, before becoming PA to their managing director. On the shop floor members of the Foster and Bancroft families gave us many years of excellent service. Derek Moore and his father, Ray, were always reliable. Michael Keeley and Gareth Hylands in the closing stages gave tremendous support to John Danks as we went through the difficult task of closing the business down.

The Danks family supported us through three generations. John's younger brother, Scott, started with us as a young lad in 1983 working in the office. He later took over responsibilities as our buyer. He was well liked and I was sorry when he left in 1994 to pursue a new career at Land Rover. His elder brother, John, had joined the company in 1977 and, after training as a toolmaker, worked in the press shop before joining us in the office where he took on the huge task of updating and standardising all our engineering drawings and hundreds of product manufacturing procedures. Later I was to appoint him first as works manager and then as general manager. Like his father, he had a special talent for getting the most out of people and creating a good working team. I was pleased to acknowledge this by appointing him as a director in 1996.

In writing this book I have come to realise how important it is to employ the best people available. I believe that amongst the great industrial cities, Birmingham has been particularly fortunate in developing a population with a tremendous work ethic, people who are prepared to work hard, often in difficult conditions, and not necessarily for the highest wage. In order to get the most out of people, it is important to create an enjoyable working environment, and I believe that in this, at least, we were successful.

Left, Denis H. Haden.

Right, John Haden.

CHAPTER SIX
Kettles, Toasters and Royal Patronage: The Creation of a Major Electrical Appliance Manufacturing Business

For the birth of something new, there has to be a happening. Isaac Newton saw an apple fall; James Watt watched a kettle boil; and these people knew enough to translate ordinary happenings into something new.

(Sir Alexander Fleming)

The Haden family cannot claim to have invented the electric kettle, but they were certainly one of the pioneers in developing reliable mechanisms for automatically switching them off, first to prevent damage to the heating element exposed through boiling dry and, in later developments, as a means of disconnecting the power as the water reached boiling point.

Earlier in this book, it was explained how the twin brothers Denis and Donald (father of the author) first became involved in the manufacture of electric kettles in 1944, and how they worked together developing markets and a product range through their associated company Bescol (Electric) Ltd. There they produced a design of kettle using the Bescol brand name, a design that was to become one of the most iconic domestic appliances of the post-war era, and a fixture of every wedding present list.

It was unfortunate that for various family reasons this arrangement did not work very well, and in 1958 the brothers decided to split and go their own ways. Denis moved to a small factory in Lancaster Street in the Gun Quarter of Birmingham to make his own kettles, creating the Haden brand name, and then in 1966 moved to much larger premises in Burntwood, Staffordshire, where there was room for expansion as the business grew. Burntwood was a well-located site as it was only a few miles

north of Birmingham, and there was a plentiful supply of female labour, particularly suitable for the many small assembly tasks associated with kettle manufacture. The old site in Lancaster Street had been compulsorily purchased for road widening and the offer of a factory in Longbridge on the south of the city had been declined due to its proximity to the Austin car factory, a high wage area.

It was at this stage that Denis, now trading as D. H. Haden Ltd., was joined by his enthusiastic young son, John, who had been educated at the famous Fettes College in Edinburgh (Tony Blair's alma mater), and then trained in accountancy. As often happens in a small but growing family business of this sort, he was expected to put his hands wherever they were needed, and so started off delivering the goods to customers himself. Later he moved to organising a formal production control system before becoming sales director.

In the Lancaster Street factory, production of aluminium kettles was limited to three hundred per day, employing twenty-five to thirty people. Other products included a limited range of saucepans with a special flanged top that prevented the water from boiling over, as well as circular strap heating elements for washing machines. The move

Haden kettles

to Burntwood enabled Denis to rapidly increase the production of kettles and by 1982 they were up to about fifteen thousand per week.

All was going well, but there was about to be a significant change in the market. Until 1982 kettles were made of chrome plated steel or aluminium, but new materials were now becoming available. Messrs British Celanese Co. developed a heat resistant plastic which they named Kemetal, especially for the kettle industry. Moulding techniques required an open top and so the modern jug-shaped kettle evolved. These were cheaper to produce, but the initial tooling cost was huge—about £200,000 for each suite of models.

Denis made the decision to go ahead and the investment proved to be worthwhile. Sales of Haden jug kettles soon overtook those of the traditional metal designs, increasing rapidly with innovations such as a sight glass on the side, cordless systems and a three-year guarantee, these Haden developments being the first in the trade.

Haden kettle, toaster and iron.

Kettle sales eventually levelled at an average of thirty thousand per week, maximum production at the height of the season once reaching eight thousand in one day. The brand name Haden had, by now, become synonymous with the words 'electric kettle'.

Following requests from customers for a wider range of Haden brand products, sales were expanded in 1984 by importing electric cordless steam irons with a Haden designed and supplied switch. These came from Messrs Solac in Spain where they were manufactured under licence. In 1988 electric toasters were added to the range—these were sourced from China. Sales of irons and toasters averaged fifty thousand each per annum.

Although the company had, by 1989, become hugely successful in generating an ever increasing demand for their products, margins were becoming tighter as a result of increased competition and a large overdraft was now causing concern. In order to raise fresh capital, D. H. Haden Ltd. converted from being a private family business (Ltd.) to being a public limited company (plc) and the West Midland Enterprise Board

(WMEB) took a 40 per cent shareholding in exchange for a substantial cash injection. For a time things continued well, but the relationship between the family and the new investors became increasingly difficult. WMEB were concerned at a fall in profits and by 1999 decided to withdraw their investment. This left the company in a difficult position and the matter could only be resolved by a sale of the assets. On 31 May 2000, the business was sold to Messrs Russell Hobbs, who moved production to other UK sites before eventually having all their kettles manufactured in China. That company was then sold on and the Haden brand name is today under American ownership.

John's father, Denis, died in 1991. With the closure of the kettle business in 2000, John was able to move on and devote his considerable energy and talent to other enterprises in which he had an interest.

Looking at the various businesses in which the Haden family has been involved over a period of more than one hundred and fifty years, there is no doubt that the manufacture of electric kettles was the most dynamic. A major domestic appliance manufacturer was created from scratch, was highly innovative and ran very successfully for a period of just over fifty years.

HRH Prince Henry of Wales (otherwise known as Prince Harry) at Eton College, 2003, playing with a Haden electric toaster – note also Haden kettle in the background.

CHAPTER SEVEN
Gregans Castle Hotel in Ireland
by Peter Haden

Peter Haden (twin brother of the author) did not enter the family business in Birmingham, but instead chose to follow a career in the hotel industry. His first management position was in an hotel in Northern Ireland where he met and, in 1965, married his wife, Moira.

In 1976 they decided to look around Ireland to find a suitable hotel to purchase. The tourist industry was in a depressed state and so hotel prices were generally low. They chose a country-house-style hotel in a remote part of the west of Ireland, on the south side of Galway Bay. Gregans Castle Hotel, at the head of a valley, had superb views and was close to the seaside village of Ballyvaughan.

The mainly nineteenth-century building, with fourteen bedrooms, was in a poor state of repair, but it had clear potential for development. The English owners had had only limited success and although the business was trading with a small profit, they wanted to sell up as fast as possible, having allegedly become best customers in their own bar. It was said that anyone complaining in the dining room was likely to have the tablecloth pulled off with everything on it!

A good deal was quickly agreed. Most of the payments would be interest-free over three years, at a time when inflation was running at up to 21 per cent. After selling their private house near Limerick at a top of

Peter Haden with his wife Moira.

Simon-Peter and his wife Frederika at an award ceremony.

Gregans Castle Hotel.

The Haden family together at the hotel.

Peter Haden in Spain on his yacht *Papageno*.

the market price and taking over the moderate hotel bank overdraft, Peter and Moira were left with sufficient funds to start improvements.

The day before signing over, one of the joint owners disappeared to England causing some panic, but he eventually returned and the deal was completed. Included in the transaction were six Shorthorn cows and a number of hens, the latter being quickly disposed of overnight by the newly-arrived family pet Basset hound.

Peter and Moira planned a change in style of business, but this could only be achieved gradually, as cash flow permitted. The existing business was heavily dependent on coach tour lunch stops and late night drinking, and the local police sergeant called to plead that something be done to respect the Licensing Law. It was clear that a choice had to be made as to what sort of business should be sought.

Enthusiastic support from the Irish Tourist Board, the AA and RAC, and personal contacts in the travel industry, together with an enormous amount of hard work by all the family, eventually paid off. The first investments were in bedroom improvements and downstairs décor and style. Peter took over all responsibility for the kitchen, while Moira not only supervised the dining room and housekeeping, but also managed their young family and gave birth to a fourth child, Alexander. In the summer holidays the older children, Simon-Peter, Christopher and Elizabeth, all made their contribution towards running the hotel. Later, Alexander went on to be captain of football at Glenstal Abbey School, Limerick, and Christopher became a senior executive with Standard Chartered Bank. Elizabeth chose a career in the media.

Following the upgrade, the Tourist Board directed some well-known travel journalists to the hotel and this produced positive results immediately, especially a dramatic rise in French and American clientele. When the British ambassador Sir Robin Haydon (no relation) chose the hotel for weekend retreats in what were then difficult political times, massive security was enforced by both the police and the army. Further patronage by many from the diplomatic corps followed, including French, Spanish, Canadian, and several American ambassadors, culminating in a holiday visit by the president of Germany, and later the foreign minister of China.

Funds continued to be ploughed back into improvements, including landscaping and the planting of many hundreds of trees. In 1991 a new wing of luxury rooms and suites designed to match the original building was built to coincide with the return from the UK and Switzerland of eldest son, Simon-Peter, who was now ready to work his way into the business. Joined by his wife, Frederika, he eventually took over in 2004.

In recent years, the hotel has been patronised by many film stars, well-known personalities and public figures. HRH Prince Charles has twice been booked in to stay, but had to cancel both times—on the first occasion because of the death of his aunt Princess Margaret, and on the second because of the outbreak of the first Gulf War.

International press accolades have continued to flow in. The hotel has become particularly well-known for its cuisine, and has been said to have the best hotel dining room in Ireland.

EPILOGUE
Et in Arcadia Ego?

What would the great industrialists of the past, Matthew Boulton, James Watt and their friends, looking out from their great manufactories in the Soho district of Birmingham today, think of the huge changes that have occurred? What thoughts would go through their minds as they observed how the noise of forges, stamping presses and steam engines has been replaced by the roar of traffic, the evening sky no longer lit by the flames of the Black Country blast furnaces, but instead by the all-pervading glare of yellow street lighting?

What would George Haden and his sons think, cycling out now to Princes End in the Black Country to meet their friends on a Sunday morning, as they had done in the 1890s, only to see the streets full of a different populace wearing strange clothes, trading goods in a scene more reminiscent of a foreign marketplace, many of the once proud Victorian factories now replaced with vast warehouses full of imported goods?

We have to wonder if they would see these fundamental changes as representing an improvement in the society that they were so instrumental in creating. The history of Birmingham is that of a once great city built by brilliant industrialists working hand in hand with an extraordinary mix of talented craftsmen, willing and capable of engaging in new ideas, new means of production, and the manufacture of new and exciting products;

indeed, it was the manufacture of goods that was so special to this area and to our forefathers.

As the years have gone by, war, conflict and depression have played their part, but more recent competition from low cost economies in the Far East has caused far more havoc and damage than any German bombing raids during the Second World War. The politicians have destroyed our secure trading links with those countries that formed part of the British Empire, and have joined us unwillingly to an ever-increasing block of foreign nations, the result of which has been a deficit in the trading of manufactured goods that continues to grow. Successive governments have failed to understand the elementary importance of the manufacturing sector, preferring instead to rely on morally questionable financial activities in the City of London.

The once great West Midlands industries of bicycle and motorcycle manufacturing have all but disappeared, along with a large number of specialised component suppliers. Many of the traditional skills associated with these industries have disappeared for ever. There is, of course, still a manufacturing industry in the area, and more recently there has been an increase in motor vehicle assembly. However, the number of engineering jobs available is considerably less than it used to be.

The period following the First World War was a time of great social change. Birmingham City Council was controlled by far thinking leaders, the most famous being Joseph Chamberlain, men with a deep social conscience anxious to seek improvements. Under their influence, a model for civic administration was created that has been adopted by cities around the world. Vast new housing estates were built, public transport and energy utility services expanded as well as the building of many new schools and hospitals—the logical outcome for a city run by Christian-minded businessmen on business principles.

Unfortunately, a study of more recent administrations will suggest that those principles have now become subsidiary to other interests. John Wyndham's apocalyptic 1951 novel *The Day of the Triffids* described horrible plants which sprouted everywhere, spreading misrule, roaming far on their roots and feasting on human flesh. Apart from the flesh-eating bit, he could well have been describing the modern day Birmingham City Council, which has more elected members than the United States Senate.

The all pervading influence of new ideologies, political correctness, and bureaucracy, together with the burden of an ever increasing multiplicity of European directives, has stifled civic and industrial development. One hundred years ago, Birmingham together with the Black Country was the manufacturing centre of the world. Today, it is but a museum of the past when compared to the many huge new vibrant cities in China where, for example, they now produce approximately eighty million bicycles each year.

Small family firms will always be tossed around by the rough seas of economic forces that prevail in a capitalist system, and they can only have a chance of survival through the hard work and enterprise of their owners. There will always be an element of luck in happening to be in the right place at the right time, so as to take advantage of new opportunities, and there will always be times when economic forces overwhelm a whole industry with devastating effect.

But despite these difficulties, the Haden family has survived, if not always through the dynastic medium of the family firm, but by moving—as had their predecessors—to seek new opportunities elsewhere in new industries at home and abroad: from glass to cycles, from kettles

Nicolas Poussin, *Les Bergers d'Arcadie*, 1637–1638, oil on canvas, Musée du Louvre.

to the hotel industry, from the Black Country to Birmingham, then to Burntwood, and on to Ballyvaughan in Ireland.

In one of the Renaissance painter Nicholas Poussin's most famous works *The Shepherds of Arcadia*, the artist depicts shepherds in a pastoral scene, resting on a tomb that bears the inscription 'Et in Arcadia Ego'. The theme of the painting is usually interpreted as meaning that it is there, in Arcadia—a utopian garden paradise in an endless summer— that the shepherds first encounter the solemn reality that all things must pass. As each generation attempts, through hard work and struggle to be successful, there will always be a realisation that death and danger are never far away.

From the dark satanic mills of nineteenth-century Wordsley and the Black Country to the green fields of the west coast of Ireland, succeeding members of the Haden family have always sought to make a contribution in their own particular way.

A bumpy ride indeed!

Donald Haden MFH (centre) with the Ledbury Hunt staff and a few favourite hounds, 1996.

The Younger Generation

Simon Peter Haden   Christopher Haden

Elizabeth Haden   Alexander Haden

Michael Stevens   Tom Stevens

APPENDIX

Transcript of a document held in Black Country Archives, Dudley, titled: 'Lease of land, premises and glass cutting shop engine house, New Street, Wordsley, Richard Mills to James Parrish, Joseph Lowe and William Haden. 1859.' Lot 46, box 9.

This Indenture made the fourteenth day of May one thousand eight hundred and fifty nine Between Richard Mills of Wordsley in the County of Stafford Glass Manufacturer of the one part and James Parrish Joseph Lowe and William Haden all of Wordsley aforesaid Master Glass Cutters and Copartners of the other part Witnesseth that the said Richard Mills doth hereby demise unto the said James Parrish Joseph Lowe and William Haden their executors administrators and assigns All that plot of land situate in New Street Wordsley aforesaid (being part and parcel of a Close of Land now or late called The Eight Lands) and containing three hundred and eighty eight superficial square yards (more or less) lately purchased by the said Richard Mills from the Mortgagee of John Jones deceased And also all and singular the Messuage Glass Cutting Shop Engine house and appurtenances standing and being thereon which said Premises were late in the occupation of Widow Jones and now of the said James Parrish Joseph Lowe and William Haden Together with the use of all and singular the Steam Engine Boiler Shafting apparatus Tackle and other articles belonging to the said Cutting Shop Engine House and

Premises hereby demised and particularly such as are mentioned and specified in the Schedule or Inventory hereunder written Together with all buildings erections fixtures ways waters privileges easements and appurtenances thereto belonging (Except and reserved unto Joseph Atkinson his heirs and assigns All and every the mines veins and seams of Coal and Ironstone in and under the said plot of Land hereby granted with power and authority to him and them to work get and dispose of the same by means of any adjoining Land he and they not being liable for any damage or injury caused to the said plot of Land expressed to be hereby demised or any erections thereon) To hold the said premises (except as aforesaid) unto the said James Parrish Joseph Lowe and William Haden their executors administrators and assigns for the term of Fourteen years from the date of these presents Rendering therefore during the said term unto the said Richard Mills his heirs and assigns the yearly rent of Thirty pounds clear of all present and future rates taxes and deductions by equal payments on the fourteenth day of August the fourteenth day of November the fourteenth day of February and the fourteenth day of May the first of such payments to be made on the fourteenth day of August next and also rendering unto the said Richard Mills his heirs and assigns on the day hereinbefore mentioned the additional yearly rent of Fifteen pounds for the Cutting Shop erections and improvements hereafter to be erected completed and made upon the said premises by the said Richard Mills in pursuance of his Covenant for that purpose hereinafter contained And the said James Parrish Joseph Lowe and William Haden hereinafter called the Lessees do hereby for themselves jointly and each of them doth hereby for himself severally and for their and each of their joint and several heirs executors administrators and assigns Covenant with the said Richard Mills his heirs and assigns that they the said Lessees their executors administrators and assigns some or one of them will during the said term pay the yearly rents hereinbefore reserved on the days and in manner aforesaid and will bear and pay all rates taxes and outgoings now payable or hereafter to become payable whether by the Landlord or Tenant in respect of the said premises And will keep the said Premises insured against loss or damage by fire in such office as the said Richard Mills his heirs or assigns shall approve in the sum of Two hundred and fifty pounds at the least and will when required produce the policy of such Insurance and the current years receipt for the premium thereon to the said Richard Mills his heirs or assigns And will once in every four years of the said term hereby granted paint twice in oil in a good and workmanlike manner all the outside and inside wood stone and ironwork of the said demised premises and other parts usually painted and will paint or colour twice in every four years the whole of the Bricks and Brickwork of the said demised Premises and other parts usually painted or coloured and will repair uphold support sustain maintain pave purge tile slate glaze paint paper whitewash colour empty cleanse amend and keep in repair the said Messuage shop Engine house buildings and premises hereby demised and all future erections buildings or improvements which shall or may be erected to or upon the said demised premises and all the walls fences gales sewers drains and other appurtenances thereto belonging in all manner of needful repairs when where and as often as occasion shall require And will repair and keep in good going trim repair and condition all the Engine Boiler Shafting apparatus tackle and other articles belonging to the said shop and Engine House and premises and particularly all such as are mentioned in the said Inventory hereinbefore mentioned And the said premises and every part thereof being in all respects so well and sufficiently repaired upheld supported sustained maintained paved purged tiled slated glazed painted papered whitewashed coloured cleansed amended fenced and kept in repair as aforesaid and the said Engine Boiler Shafting Machinery apparatus tackle and other articles and things in such good going trim repair and condition as aforesaid shall and will at the end or other sooner determination of the said term which shall first happen peaceably leave surrender and yield up until the said Richard Mills his heirs or assigns Together with all and singular the door locks keys bolts bars and other fastenings chimney pieces ranges slabs footpaces windows window shutters partitions shelves pumps water pipes posts gates and every other thing which now are or shall hereafter during the said term be affixed to set up upon made part of or belonging to the said hereby demised premises or any future erections or buildings thereon And moreover that it shall be lawful for the said Richard Mills his heirs or assigns without any notice of his intention so to do and with or without workmen and servants at all seasonable times in the day to enter upon the said demised premises and to view the state and condition of the same and of all decays and wants of reparation and amendment which upon every such view shall be found to give or leave notice in writing on the said demised premises to repair and amend the same within one Calendar month then next ensuing within which time after such notice the said Lessees their executors administrators or assigns shall repair and amend the same under the inspection of and in such manner as shall be approved by the said Richard Mills his heirs or assigns or such person as shall be appointed by him or them for that purpose and in default thereof it shall be lawful for the said Richard Mills his heirs or assigns to repair and amend all such defaults and want of reparations whereof such notice shall be so given as aforesaid and to charge the said Lessees their executors administrators and assigns with the costs and expenses of such repairs and amendments as and by way of additional rent with full power and liberty to enter upon and recover the same by distress on the said premises as for rent in arrear And also that they the said Lessees their executors or administrators or assigns will not at any time during the said term alter or injure or cause to or permit to be altered or injured the said demised premises or any part thereof or assign or underlet or otherwise part with this Indenture of Lease or the premises thereby demised nor sell dispose of or otherwise part with or remove therefrom any of the household furniture goods chattels property and effects in upon or about the said demised premises belonging to them the said Lessees and used in their business as Glass Cutters (particularly the following (that is to say) Seven Glass Cutters and Troughs Frames Eight Bands two stopping lathes and Glass Cutters Tools consisting of Mills Stones Spindles and pulleys without the permission in writing of the said Richard Mills his heirs and assigns for all or any of the purposes aforesaid first had and obtained Provided always and it is hereby agreed between the said parties hereto that on any breach or non observance of any of the Covenants herein contained the said Richard Mills his heirs or assigns may enter upon the said demised premises and seize and distrain upon the several articles and property belonging to the said Lessees their executors administrators and assigns and about the said demised premises and every distress there made take away and retain to his and their use And sell the distress as in common cases of distress for rent and out of the money arising thereby retain any rent money due or to become due and the cost of making keeping and selling such distress and on every such failure as aforesaid or if the premises hereby demised shall be assigned or assignable by means of the Bankruptcy or Insolvency of the said Lessees their executors administrators or assigns the said Richard Mills his heirs or assigns may re enter and enjoy the premises hereby demised as if these presents had not be executed or at his or their option keep these presents in force and increase the rent of the Premises hereby dismissed in the proportion of ten pounds per centum upon the amount of the rental hereby reserved and until any such failure or until the said premises shall be assigned or assignable as aforesaid the said Lessees their executors administrators may enjoy the said premises without eviction or (except as hereinbefore excepted and reserved) interruption by the said Richard Mills his heirs or assigns And the said Richard Mills doth hereby for himself his heirs executors and administrators covenant with the said Lessees their executors administrators and assigns that he will within a reasonable time from the date of these presents provided the Covenants on the part of the said Lessees their executors administrators and assigns herein contained shall be fully performed and kept at his own cost build new Cutting Shops on the said demised premises or enlarge the Cutting Shops now being thereon and complete the same with all the usual and customary Shafting apparatus and other things usual for Glass Cutters making the same of such size and dimensions as to afford sufficient room and accommodation for fourteen more frames In witness whereof the said parties to these presents have hereunto set their hands and seals the day and year first above written

The Schedule above referred to
House sealed tiled glazed painted in good repair and complete with Pump Water Cistern, Kitchen, Parlour, Brewhouse, three bedrooms, Cellar with Spouting Windows.

Boiler in good repair with stop valve, buoy, doors and grate damper chain and Weight Fittings Four Buckstaffs complete.

Engine House, Eight horse Engine, New Metallic Piston, Flywheel, governors Pulleys, Two brass Excentries, Brass Slides, Valves, piping, Motion Rods for Pumps with gearing for ditto, Iron plate over Cistern and Buoy chain and weight complete in good efficient working order.

First cutting shop Door shaft with nine Pullies three jowinies one Coupling Box Shelving on two sides Stopperers Framework, Four small shelves, Composition driving-band Cross pieces and lintels.

New Shop Door, New Shafting with three pulleys and two driving ditto, Three Jowinies, One Coupling Box and Composition driving bank, Turning Lathe Dog and Rest, Two shelves on one side of Shop, Railing before Flywheel.

Lintels Cross pieces complete.

[Signed and sealed by]

James Parrish

Joseph Lowe

William Haden

The velocipede has its 'poet', as witness the following from *The Velocipedist*:

She saw him en velocipede
A-kitting up the road
And pitty-pat and patty-pit
Her little heartlet goed,
And soft she sobbered to herself,
"Though fast his paces be,
He cannot dust so quick but what
My heart keeps up with he.

"O, vive la belle velocipede !
Which digs along the street;
But that which I do chiefly vive
Is he who does the feat.
I cannot help a loving him,
Nor he help loving me;
Velocipedestrination is
A thing that has to be."

Etiquette for a velocipede rider (circa 1864)

We had almost forgotten to say something about the "civil rule of the road". A Western (U.S.) journal comes to the rescue in manner following :-

"If a fellow goes with his velocipede to call upon a lady, whose house has no front yard, and no back yard, and there is a lot of boys in front of it ready to pounce upon his machine, and the lady is smiling through the window, what is he to do with it ?

If a fellow riding his velocipede, meets a lady on a particularly rough bit of road, where it requires both hands to steer, is he positively required to let go with one hand to lift his hat; and if so, what will he do with his machine ?

If a fellow, riding his velocipede, overtakes a lady carrying two bundles and a parcel, what should he do with it ?

If a fellow, riding his machine, meets three ladies walking abreast, opposite a particularly tall curb stone, what ought he to do with it ?

If a lady meets a fellow riding his machine, and asks her to go shopping with her, what can he do with it ?

If the hind wheel of a fellow's machine flings mud just above the saddle, ought he to call on people who do not keep a duplex mirror and a clothes-brush in the front hall ?

If a fellow, riding his velocipede, encounters his expected father-in-law, bothering painfully over a bit of slippery side-walk, what shall he do with it ?

If people coming suddenly round corners, will run against a fellow's machine, is he bound to stop and apologise, or are they ?

If a fellow is invited to join a funeral procession, ought he to ride his machine ?

And is it proper to ride a velocipede to church; and if so, what will he do with it when he gets there ?"

To this he says there should be a "mixed commission" of ladies to decide these matters.

Crosby & Mayer 1899 catalogue

INTRODUCTION During the season just passed, the volume of business ●●●●·· done by our factory has been the largest in its history, and we wish to take this opportunity of thanking our many friends for their generous patronage. That we may deserve a continuance of your favor it is our constant aim so to conduct the details of the manufacturing, selling and delivery of our goods as to satisfy the most exacting requirements. We make no secret of the pleasure it has given us to receive from time to time expressions of much satisfaction with the manner in which orders have been filled—not only with regard to the high quality of our stampings but to our exceptionally prompt delivery of them. If a manufacturer of bicycles cannot get his parts *when* he wants them, it matters little whether the parts themselves are good, bad or indifferent. We have always put particular stress on this matter of delivery, and the extensive alterations in our factory during a two-weeks' shutdown this summer had this object especially in view. At that time a new power plant of nearly twice the horse-power of the old was installed, a number of heavy special presses were set up, and new case-hardening and annealing furnaces were added. With these improvements we are today in better position than ever to get out work accurately and rapidly.

The making of bicycle frame connections from sheet steel is an industry of comparatively recent development but of very rapid growth, and from its earliest beginnings the officers of our company have been closely identified with its progress. Indeed, the first stampings of this character ever offered to the trade were made by a company, of which our President was General Manager.

A glance through the lists of parts shown on succeeding pages will indicate how fully and completely all demands of the trade may be met today. Our lines include parts for nearly every possible combination: for outside joint or flush joint frames; for $1\frac{1}{4}$ or $1\frac{1}{8}$ in. tubing; for $2\frac{1}{2}$, 3 or 4 in. drop at hanger; for 28 or 30 in. wheels; for seat-post clusters adapted for expanders, or the ordinary bolt and nut clamp; for double rear stays or single lug; for one-piece heads for 22, 23, 24, 25, 26 or 27 in. frames, or separate head lugs for any odd heights desired. To these add a full line of handle-bar and seat-post tees made for both the American and foreign standards; a varied line of rear fork-ends and adjustments, among which our new patented adjustment is particularly worthy of your attention; and crowns, head fittings and frame braces of approved designs, and you have the most complete assortment of these goods on the market.

We also make many special pieces to order and are in position to figure to advantage on any work in stamped sheet steel.

For the products of the other factories herein catalogued we ask the trade's careful consideration. These goods have been chosen by us to complete our lines on the basis of quality and merit combined with fair prices.

CROSBY & MAYER CO.

BUFFALO, N. Y., Dec. 1st, 1898.

If it's to be made of sheet steel send it to us.

**Some of the motorcycle technical features pioneered by Alfred Haden
1903–1931**

He was the first to introduce the bent top rail allowing seat height
adjustment to suit all sizes of riders.

He was the first British manufacturer to build frames with a single
piece two-way head lug.

On some models a two-speed (later three-speed) chain driven gearbox
was optional.

Universal frame engine mounting brackets with a variety of hole
positions and sizes were brazed to the seat and down tubes, thereby
allowing different engines to be fitted in a standard frame.

The Colonial model first introduced in 1912 had an unusual rear brake
operated by the foot on the belt rim and was available with the sidecar
mounted on the right-handed side for continental roads.

In about 1912 Alfred patented a system for lubricating the two-stroke
engine through a sight fed oil pump.

On these earlier models a special rear carrier was built on the frame
leaving the saddle springs clear for low position and leaving space for
snugly fitted pannier bags.

The Haden designed and manufactured single cylinder 'Climax' engine
introduced in 1914 had several special features. In particular it had a rather
distinctive shape of cylinder block featuring a reduction in the size of the
radiating fins from top to bottom in wedge formation and a pair of cast
iron flywheels mounted inside the crankcase. This engine was successfully
proven in the 1921 and 1922 TT Races.

Haden New Comet motorcycle developments

1905–1909: Single cylinder and V-Twin engine models were developed using various engines including Zedel and Peugeot.
Ladies models were included in the range.

1910: Sarolea, JAP and Peugeot engines were introduced.

1911: Precision singles were added to the range.

1912: All engines were by Precision. Models included a lightweight and a Colonial which were also sold as the Comet-Precision.

1913: There was a model with a JAP engine.

Later, after taking over the firm of Regal Green in 1913, they began to fit the water-cooled Green engine. It seems probable that the acquisition of Regal Green's special machinery, which was needed to manufacture engines, had enabled Alfred to now go ahead with his own ideas on engine design.

1914: Introduction of the innovative Haden designed and manufactured Climax two-stroke engine with distinctive cylinder shape and internal flywheels.

1914–1916: A 219cc two-stroke was introduced with the additional option of a two-speed gearbox and Druid forks. There was also a 349cc version. Post-war machines included a 292cc two-stroke and a 499cc four-stroke.

1920: Only two-stroke machines were produced.

1921: 269cc model with Villiers Mark 3 engine and Haden Climax 293cc engine models were listed. A Government Regulation at this time reduced by half the tax paid if a motorcycle weighed less than 200lbs. The New Comet with Haden Climax engine weighed only 154lbs.

1923: Re-launch of the improved New Comet Light Touring Combination, expressly designed as a low cost passenger vehicle providing an ideal and economical form of motoring for not just 'about town' use but also for touring purposes. The Haden manufactured engine with internal flywheels used in this motorcycle combination was sold under the slogan 'The machine with the heart in the right place'.

1924: A version with a 147cc JAP Aza engine was added to the range.

1925: More versions of this model were listed.

1926-1927: Only one version of the 147cc was listed.

1928: There was just a 172cc Super Sports model with three-speed gearbox.

1931: A new 196cc Super Sports model was introduced but it was the last year of manufacture.

All models produced had belt drive to the rear wheel.

Some technical notes on motorcycle side-cars

Side-cars first appeared in about 1903 and remained the most popular means of family and commercial transport until the 1920s when affordable cars and small vans became available. They were typically manufactured to fit on a tubular steel chassis rigidly fixed onto one side to the motorcycle with a body then mounted on to provide passenger seating or alternatively a compartment to carry goods. The bodies usually consisted of an ash wooden frame enclosed with steel or plywood sheeting. For extra lightness the body was sometimes made from woven basketwork.

The driving sensation is completely different to that of a solo machine and unless there is a brake on the non-driven side-car wheel it will pull towards the bike under braking, and conversely the bike towards the side-car under acceleration. Driver and passenger body position also affect higher speed handling on uneven roads and it is necessary therefore to co-ordinate the geometry of both units to give some stability.

The steering geometry of the motorcycle will have been originally set up for a tilting single track vehicle and it is necessary for side-car use to change this to turn slightly away from the drag imposed by the side-car. This can be achieved by clamping the motorcycle rigidly a few degrees opposite the side-car and additionally setting up a few degrees of toe-in of the side-car wheel towards the centreline of the combination. This will assist in providing a balance resulting in a more comfortable ride and a straighter line of travel.

Patents

Bibliographic data: GB664885 (A) — 1952-01-16

Improvements relating to the manufacture of cycle handle-bar lugs

Inventor(s):

Applicant(s):   DONALD WILLIAM HADEN; DENIS HOWARD HADEN ± (DONALD
                 WILLIAM HADEN, ; DENIS HOWARD HADEN)

Classification: - international: *B21D53/86*
                 - cooperative: *B21D53/86*

Application   GB19490023776 19490915
number:

Priority   GB19490023776 19490915
number(s):

Abstract of GB664885 (A)

664,885. Making handle-bar lugs.
HADEN, D. W., and HADEN, D. H. Aug.
1, 1950 [Sept. 15, 1949], No. 23776/49.
Class 83 (ii). A cycle handle-bar formed
by bending at about the middle a single
metal pressing to cause shaped or
flanged end portions to come together to
complete a hollow structure having a
transverse through passage for the
handlebar, one of the end portions being
apertured to receive a handle-bar stem

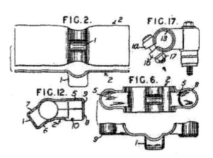

and the join of the two end portions being welded or brazed together the middle of the
hollow structure being recessed is then divided to form a pair of lugs which are bolted
together to adjustably grip the handle-bar. The metal blank 2, as shown in Fig. 2, has a
pressed out part 1. The two end parts 5 are shaped, Fig. 6, and holes 6 and 7, Fig. 12
are made in the part 1. The end parts 5 are flanged and an opening 10 is cut in the end
8. The parts 8 and 9 are brought together, Fig. 12, and brazed or welded to form the
lug for the handle-bar stem and an aperture for. the handle-bar which is provided with a
liner 13, Fig. 17. The part 1 is split to form lugs 1a, 1b, through which passes a bolt with
a nut 17 to adjustably secure the handle-bar. In modifications the lug may have a
triangular form in a vertical or horizontal plane or by extending the blank the handlebars may be offset from the handle-bar stem.

Bibliographic data: GB803024 (A) — 1958-10-15

Improvements relating to clips, particularly bicycle handle-bar clips

Inventor(s):	HADEN DONALD WILLIAM ± (HADEN DONALD WILLIAM)
Applicant(s):	HADEN BROS LTD ± (HADEN BROS. LIMITED)
Classification:	- international: *B62K21/12*
	- cooperative: B62K21/12
Application number:	GB19560001930 19560120
Priority number(s):	GB19560001930 19560120

Abstract of GB803024 (A)

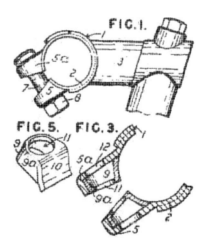

FIG. 1. FIG. 5. FIG. 3.

803,024. Handle bars. HADEN BROS., Ltd. Dec. 6, 1956 [Jan. 20, 1956], No. 1930/56. Class 136(3) [Also in Group XXV] A band clip 1 comprises a split band 2 having a pair of outwardly projecting D-shaped hollow ears 5 and 5a which are apertured at 12 to receive a clamping nut and bolt 8, 7 and have a U-shaped wall with the inside of the ears 5 and 5a opening into the interior of the band 2; D-shaped liners 9, Fig. 5, fit into the ears 5 and 5a to prevent them collapsing when the band is tightened. The liner 9, formed from a sheet metal blank, consists of a U-shaped wall 9a and a cross-piece 10, the liner being inverted in the ear 5 with the bottom of the liner uppermost and formed with a bolt hole 11 opposite to hole 12. The cross-piece 10 rigidly connects the walls of the ear 5 and is curved to follow the curvature of the inner face of the band 2, any gaps between the cross-piece 10 and band 2 may be filled with welding metal and the liner may be fixed to the ear by welding, brazing, soldering, &c. In Fig. 8 (not shown), the liner is fitted with its bolt hole and the bolt hole in the ear coinciding, i.e.' the liner is not inverted. The liner of Figs. 9 and 10 (not shown) is a flat D-shaped plate with a plate-like extension similar to the cross-piece 10. The clip is shown in Fig. 1 in use for attaching a bicycle handlebar to the bracket 3 but this use is not exclusive.

Bibliographic data: GB863449 (A) — 1961-03-22

Improvements relating to handlebar stems for bicycles

Inventor(s):	HADEN DONALD WILLIAM ± (HADEN DONALD WILLIAM)
Applicant(s):	HADEN BROS LTD ± (HADEN BROS. LIMITED)
Classification:	- international: *B62K21/12* - cooperative: <u>B62K21/12</u>
Application number:	GB19590002561 19590123
Priority number(s):	GB19590002561 19590123

Abstract of GB863449 (A)

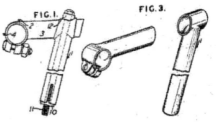

863,449. Handlebars. HADEN BROS. Ltd. Jan. 5, 1960 [Jan. 23, 1959], No. 2561/59. Class 136(3). A cycle handlebar stem tube 1 carries a transversely-extending lug 2 which is formed as a one-piece casting from malleable iron and consists of a tubular part 3 formed at one end with a tubular clip 4 adapted for clamping around the handlebar, the upper end of the stem tube 1 being fashioned to embrace a portion of the tubular part of the lug and being brazed, soldered or welded thereto. The stem tube may be hollow to receive a headed bolt 11 carrying an expander cone 10. This bolt passes through the tubular part 3 of the lug and through boss or shaped washer 12.

Bibliographic data: GB899129 (A) — 1962-06-20

Improvements relating to pedal cycle components, particularly cycle fork crowns, and to their method of manufacture

Inventor(s):	HADEN DONALD WILLIAM ± (HADEN DONALD WILLIAM)
Applicant(s):	HADEN BROS LTD ± (HADEN BROS. LIMITED)

Classification:	- international:	*B21D53/86*
	- cooperative:	<u>*B21D53/86*</u>

Application number: GB19610004289 19610204

Priority number(s): GB19610004289 19610204

Abstract of GB899129 (A)

899,129. Making cycle parts; stamping. HADEN BROS. Ltd. Feb. 4, 1961, No. 4289/61. Classes 83 (2) and 83 (4). The radiused edges of a cycle fork crown are formed as square cut corners by the method of placing the crown between two dies and upsetting the metal of the crown into the corners of one die. One die comprises blocks 11, 13 and 16, a sharp corner being formed at 15, and the ram-operated block 16 including an ejector 17. A block 7 forms the lower die, the finished crown 1 with square cut corners 5 being shown in Fig. 6.

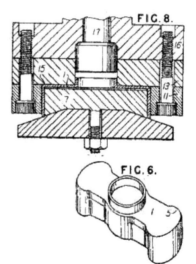

FIG. 8.

FIG. 6.

Some notes on the method of manufacturing cycle frame components as used in the Haden cycle component factory

A traditional diamond shaped bicycle frame consists of a set of tubes joined together at the corners with connecting pieces known as frame lugs. The tubes at the lower joint are connected together with a bottom bracket shell. These parts are assembled and brazed together before shot-blasting and painting. This was always the most common means of production until the 1980s when improved welding technology and new alloy steels made it possible to introduce new frame designs without the need for connecting pieces.

Frame lugs are manufactured from sheet steel blanks carefully formed in specially shaped press tools and then gas welded along the upper and lower seams before being machined inside both bores so as to provide an accurate sliding fit over the frame tubes. The fit is important so as to allow ease of assembly and to provide a good brazing joint. Using special jigs, the angle between the pipes can be accurately controlled during the machining process. Subsequently the more intricate outline in the front and pipe ends of the lug are cut using special tools in hand operated presses. This operation is known as 'feature cutting'.

The idea of manufacturing frame lugs in this way is believed to have been pioneered in America in the early 1890s by a Mr William H Crosby, who later set up his own business in Buffalo, New York State, trading as Crosby & Mayer Co. His company's marketing slogan was 'If it's to be made of sheet steel send it to us' and they made an extensive range of bicycle parts. The company still exists and is now managed and owned by the grandson of the founder. They no longer have any connection with the bicycle industry but instead make pressed steel parts for the motor vehicle industry.

It was in about 1892 that Raleigh in Nottingham adopted from America this means of production and were probably the first in the UK to do so. Alfred Haden was to follow soon after having up until then manufactured frame lugs by the original method – machining raw malleable whiteheart steel castings produced in a local foundry to his own design – a method still used by Haden Bros Ltd right through to the year 2002 where special strong parts were required for heavy duty and other types of tradesmen's cycles.

Haden bottom bracket shells were generally made as machined whiteheart castings but later produced from steel tube–a process adopted in 1978 using Japanese technology known as bulge forming. The essence of this method is that of taking a piece of steel tube approximately three inches long and an inch and a half in diameter, snugly fitting inside a piece of rubber of the same internal dimensions and then, in a two hundred tonne hydraulic power press, compressing both ends in an enclosed set of tools. As the tube reduces in length the rubber expands and cause the walls to bulge into cavities in the walls of the press tool allowing four domes to form on the outside. In subsequent press operations these domes are opened up and become the pipes into which the frame tubes and chainstays can be assembled.

Fork crowns were made as machined whiteheart steel castings for heavy duty cycles and as steel pressings for normal bikes. The pressed type usually consisted of an outer shell made from deep drawing quality steel into which is fitted a pressed steel liner–a complex pressing with an inner tubular shape into which is later brazed the bicycle steering column.

Fork crowns were manufactured in many shapes and sizes. This was because bicycle designers liked to specify a unique shape so as to identify their own brand or model. The most famous of these was the Raleigh tubular crown, designed to look like a horizontal piece of tube but in fact made from a flat piece of steel. These were made by Raleigh in their own press shop, but following the closure of much of their manufacturing facility in Nottingham in 1990, production was subcontracted to Hadens.

Manufacturing cycle frame lugs

The first production stage.

A 16 swg mild steel blank, ready to be formed into a bicycle gent's top head lug (not to scale).

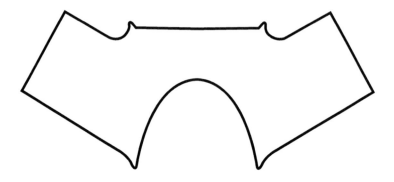

The final machining operation before 'feature cutting'.

Measuring Frame and Lug Angles

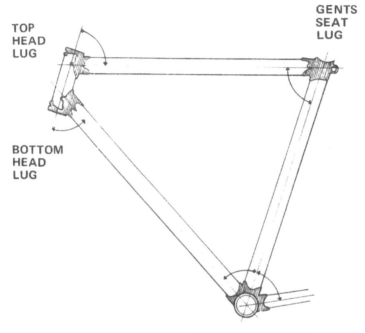

The above was addressed: 'To Donald W. Haden with good wishes Johnny Helms.'

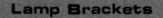

Lamp Brackets HADEN

D23 STANDARD PATTERN
for 1" columns.

D27 STANDARD PATTERN
for 1" column with tag.

D21 GIRDER TYPE
for 1" columns.

D28 FOR FRONT FORK FITTING
with serrated side face.
*Available for left hand or
right hand fork fitting.*

*All components supplied with
chrome finish.*

HADEN STEEL BOTTOM BRACKETS

HADEN SPORTS BOTTOM BRACKET
V. Pattern (for straight stays)

If required brackets can be supplied
with three weight saving slots cut in
the underside.

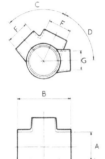

Catalogue Reference	Thread for Cup A	Width B	Angle C	Angle D	E	F	G
VBS5964	1.370'' x 24 TPI	68	59°	64°	38	28.6	22.2
VBS6061	1.370'' x 24 TPI	68	60°	61°	38	28.6	22.2
VBS6162	1.370'' x 24 TPI	68	61°	62°	38	28.6	22.2
VBS6164	1.370'' x 24 TPI	68	61°	64°	38	28.6	22.2
VBS6262	1.370'' x 24 TPI	68	62°	62°	38	28.6	22.2
VBS6363	1.370'' x 24 TPI	68	63°	63°	38	28.6	22.2
VBS6461	1.370'' x 24 TPI	68	64°	61°	38	28.6	22.2
VBS6462	1.370'' x 24 TPI	68	64°	62°	38	28.6	22.2

Extension Tips for welding onto pipes are available if required — see page 17

Type HM1 for welded frames
1.370'' x 24 TPI BSC Thread
68mm wide 3 mm wall thickness.

Type HM2 for welded frame
1.370 x 24 TPI BSC Thread
68mm wide.
Chainstay pipes 22.2mm I/D
38mm between centres.

15

HADEN FORK CROWNS

EUROPA

This crown is a precision made component accurately machined from a high Quality Steel Investment casting.

Separate extension tangs are available if required. See page 17.

This crown has been specially designed for use with Reynolds New Continental oval section blades.

It is also suitable for Columbus Italian oval and Super Vitus European oval fork blades.

20 mm

27.5 mm

TRACK

This is a sturdy ultra lightweight steel fork crown for round section track fork blades.

22.2 mm

CROWN ref HTC222

OVAL SPORTS

Attractive pressed steel fork crown to suit most normal requirements.

A choice of cut-out designs are available as illustrated.

This Crown is accurately sized to accept standard European fork blades 16 x 29mm oval section.

16 mm

29 mm

HCN.7S   HCN.8   HCN.9   HCN.10   HCN.11   HCN.12

Matching Chromium plated fork crown covers or Top Plates are available to suit, if required.

16

POLARIS Lug Sets

The ultimately simple classical design

POLARIS design P101

TOP HEAD LUG

SEAT LUG

BOTTOM HEAD LUG

BOTTOM BRACKET

Special design features.
Clean Simple Line

POLARIS design P102

TOP HEAD LUG

SEAT LUG

BOTTOM HEAD LUG

BOTTOM BRACKET

Special design features.
As P101 but incorporating
triangular cut outs in body

POLARIS design P103

TOP HEAD LUG

SEAT LUG

BOTTOM HEAD LUG

BOTTOM BRACKET

Special design features.
As P102 but incorporating
triangular cut outs in top
of pipes.

Components illustrated above are available to the following Specifications					
ITEM	**INSIDE DIAMETERS**	**ANGLES AVAILABLE**			
TOP HEAD LUG	31.8mm x 25.4mm	72	72	73	73
BOTTOM HEAD LUG	31.8mm x 28.6mm	60	61	59	59
SEAT LUG	28.6mm x 25.4mm	72	72	73	74
BOTTOM BRACKET	28.6 x 28.6 x 22.2mm	Various Types available see page 15			
FORK CROWN	25.4mm	Various Types available see page 16			

All Lugs are fully
machined to ensure
accurate angles
and bore sizes

When ordering Lugs
and Bottom Brackets
please state carefully
the angles required.
Lugs can be
ordered as separate
items or in sets.

5

Context

Some of the social, cultural and technological changes that occurred during the 1980s coinciding with a period of rapid decline in the UK bicycle manufacturing industry.

Dawn of the yuppie.
Rampant materialism promoted by the Thatcher government.
War broke out between Iran and Iraq.
John Lennon was murdered in New York.
No more free milk in schools.
Wedding of Prince Charles and Lady Diana Spencer.
The Falklands War.
The Berlin Wall was demolished.
The film *ET* was released.
The Miners' Strike.
One in ten unemployed.
Lockerbie flight bombing.
Chernobyl nuclear disaster.
IBM produce its first PC in the USA.
Rubik's Cube launched.
Microwaves gained popularity in the home.
Camcorder developed by Sony.
Compact Disc players developed.
Mobile cellular phones became popular.
Introduction of the Haden Jug Kettle.
Apple introduced the Macintosh computer.
ZX81 personal computer launched by Clive Sinclair.
Following on from BMX, mountain bikes became a new craze.
Mass import of cheap bikes from the Far East.
Digital watches and personal Walkmans became popular.

Independent UK bicycle manufacturers at the time of the merger of J. A. Phillips with Raleigh in 1962 (excluding small lightweight builders)

Birmingham Bicycle Co. (later trading as Halmanco in South Wales).

Brown Bros. (Vindec brand later made for them by Comrade).

Comrade Cycle Co. (the largest of the independents, closed 1987).

CWS Cycle Co. (Co-op factory in Tyseley, Birmingham made Post Office cycles).

Coventry Eagle Cycle and Motor Co. (Douglas Mayo's business trading as Falcon cycles).

Dawes Cycles (family business, later part of Tandem/Falcon group).

Elswick Hopper Cycle and Motor Co. (most of their cycles were made by Raleigh).

The Enfield Cycle Co. Ltd. ('Royal Enfield' Redditch, closed 1967).

Holdsworthy in London (sold to Elswick Hopper mid 1980s).

Kirk and Merrifield – (Trading as Swift Cycles).

Leonard Gundle Cycles (closed 1974 following death of proprietor).

Norman Cycles – Ashford, Kent.

W. R. Pashley Ltd. (took over Gundles).

The Standard Cycle Co Ltd (Birmingham family business closed in 1970s)

Trusty Manufacturing Co. (later trading as Trusty Viscount).

Unique and Unity (made Triang cycles and mini Moulton, factory sold to Raleigh 1971).

Viking Cycles (closed in 1967 but re-launched in 1976 in Northern Ireland).

Wearwell Cycle Co (sold to Elswick Hopper in about 1969).

Manufacturers who started up later

Arden Cycles (registered 1977).

Bickerton (manufactured in UK 1971–1989).

Brompton Bicycle Ltd. (started 1988).

Hawk Cycles Ltd., Cradley Heath (started in 1968).

Lew Ways Ltd (adult bicycles circa 1980).

Micro Cycles Ltd. (Peter Radnall 1976).

Moulton Bicycles (1962-1967 as a major manufacturer).

Orbit Cycles (started circa 1980).

Townsend Cycles (started late-1970s)

UK cycle component and accessory manufacturers after 1962

Accles and Pollock Ltd.

Adcal Labels Ltd.

C. J. Adie and Nephew Ltd. (closed 1990)

Andrew Hague Co.

Bantel Co.

Baycliffe Co.

Bayliss Wiley and Co. Ltd.

Blumel Bros. Ltd.

British Hub Co. Ltd.

J. B. Brooks and Co. (incorporating Wrights and Lycett Saddles)

Carradice of Nelson Ltd.

S. J. Clarkes Cables Ltd.

Chater-Lea Ltd.

Cyclo Gear Co. Ltd.

T. D. Cross and Sons Ltd.

Davis Components Ltd.

Dixon Vaughan Ltd (taken over by Haden Bros Ltd in 1982)

Dunlop Rubber Co Ltd.

Fibrax Ltd.

GB Cycle Components Ltd.

Gills Cables Ltd.

Haden Bros. Ltd.

Karrimor Ltd.

Lemet (spokes and nipples)

Middlemores (Coventry) Ltd.

Midland Gearcase Co.

Midland Wheel Co.

H. Miller and Co. Ltd.

E. Nicklin and Sons (incorporating Williams Chainwheels from 1963)

J. A. Phillips and Co. Ltd.

E. A. Radnall Ltd.

Reynolds Chains Ltd.

TI Reynolds Ltd.

Royce Racing

Spencer Manufacturing Ltd.

TI Sturmey-Archer Ltd.

TI Tube Products Ltd.

Wilkinson Wheel Co. Ltd.

Overseas countries to which Haden Bros Ltd exported

Angola	Japan
Australia	Mexico
Austria	Netherlands
Belgium	Nigeria
Brazil	New Zealand
Canada	Norway
Colombia	Portugal
Denmark	Rhodesia (Zimbabwe)
Finland	South Africa
France	Spain
Germany	Sri Lanka (Ceylon)
Northern Ireland	Sweden
Republic of Ireland	Switzerland
Israel	USA
Italy	Venezuela
Jamaica	

MOULTON BICYCLES
Celebrating 50 Years
1962 - 2012

Dr Alex Moulton, C.B.E., R.D.I, FREng., Mr Shaun Moulton &

The Moulton Bicycle Company

INVITE

Mr Haden + guest

to celebrate The 50th Anniversary of the Moulton Bicycle

on Friday, 9th November from 2 - 5 p.m.

at The Hall, Holt Road, Bradford on Avon, BA15 1AJ

R.S.V.P
Shaun Moulton
The Moulton Bicycle Company
Holt Road
Bradford on Avon
BA15 1AH
Tel: 01225 865895   Dress Code: Smart Casual
Email: office@moultonbicycles.co.uk   Parking: available at the Moulton Bicycle Company

Bibliographic data: GB562997 (A) — 1944-07-25

Improvements in electric immersion heaters

Inventor(s):

Applicant(s):   CECIL BERTRAM ANNABLE ± (CECIL BERTRAM ANNABLE)

Classification: - international: H05B1/02
                - cooperative: H05B1/0213

Application number: GB19430003800 19430309

Priority number(s):   GB19430003800 19430309

Abstract of GB562997 (A)

562,997. Electric immersion heaters. ANNABLE, C. B. March 9, 1943, Nos. 3800 and 9405. [Class 64 (ii)] [Also in Groups XI and XXXVII] A thermostatically controlled electric immersion heater suitable for a kettle comprises a metal sheath 3 containing a coiled resistance wire or tape 2 bent into a loop the ends of which pass through a metal socket 4 in the wall of the kettle. One end of the resistance is connected to a contact pin 6, and the other to a similar pin 7 through a thermal switch. The contact 8 of the switch is carried by a spring blade 10 attached to a metal plate 11 secured to the pin 7, and the other contact 9 is carried by a metal plate 13 secured to an insulating plug 5, and connected to the resistance. A bimetallic strip 15 is housed in a metal tube 16 flattened at its outer end 16a to which the strip is brazed, the tube being brazed or welded to the metal

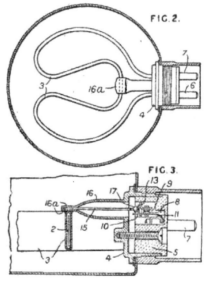

FIG. 2.

FIG. 3.

sheath 3 at a re-entrant loop. An insulating ball 17 actuates the switch. The tube 16 may be of square section, and the strip 15 may be carried by a plug fitting its end.

Bibliographic data: GB752468 (A) — 1956-07-11

Improvements in electric immersion heaters

Inventor(s):	ANNABLE CECIL BERTRAM ± (ANNABLE CECIL BERTRAM)
Applicant(s):	BESCOL ELECTRIC LTD ± (BESCOL (ELECTRIC) LIMITED)

Classification:	- international:	*H05B1/02*
	- cooperative:	H05B1/0213

Application number: GB19540005657 19540226

Priority number(s): GB19540005657 19540226

Abstract of GB752468 (A)

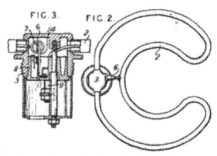

752,468. Thermal switches. BESCOL (ELECTRIC), Ltd. Feb. 24, 1955 [Feb. 26, 1954], No. 5657/54. Class 38(5) [Also in Group XI] A thermostatically controlled immersion heater is adapted for use in washing machines and other water containers having downwardly extending terminals or contact pins. As shown, a sheathed wire heating element 2 has its ends secured in an inverted cup-shaped casing 3 into which an open end of a tube 6 containing a bimetallic strip 7 projects, the other tube end being closed by flattening a,nd welded to the sheath of the element 2. The bimetallic strip is secured at one end by being clamped between the flattened sides of the tube 6 and its other end projects into the casing 3 where it engages an insulated extension 14 of a spring contact blade 11 mounted on an insulating plug 8 carrying terminals 9. Specification 562,997 is referred to.

Haden patent, February 1981, EP 0024130 A1

Inventor: Denis Howard Haden

Applicant: D. H. Haden Ltd.

Electric Kettle
EP 0024130 A1

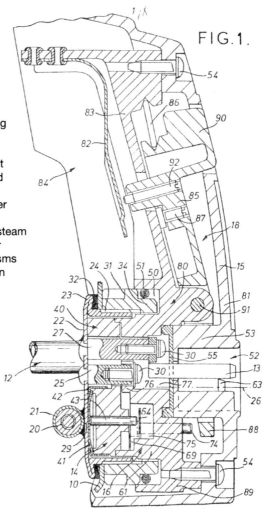

FIG.1.

An electric kettle having a metal sheathed element (20) permanently mounted on a metal head (22) so as to produce a hot spot (29) and the switching means comprising a dry overload responsive actuating mechanism 14 responsive to overheating of the hot spot to open switch contacts (71,72) mounted on an electrical insulating mounting (61) which supports a movable thrust member (74) which extends from the contacts through a way within the mounting to a steam responsive actuating mechanism (18) for actuation by the latter, and the mechanisms (14) and (18) are preferably assembled on the mounting (61) to form an assembly in which the contacts are disposed in a chamber (75) within the assembly.

Author's note: This illustration shows the complexity, not often realised, of the design and construction of an electric kettle switching mechanism.

Haden patent, May 1997, US 5895595 A
Inventor: John Denis Haden
Original Assignee: D. H. Haden Plc.

Apparatus for making beverages

The apparatus for making beverages comprises a kettle 15, a stand 10 and separable electrical connector means 16a, b to automatically connect the kettle with an electrical power supply connector in the stand when the kettle is placed on the stand; the stand is extended and provides a platform for a pot 13 and an electric heating member 14 is provided to heat a vessel on the platform alongside the kettle, and is provided with switch means to selectively energize the heating member and/or the kettle.

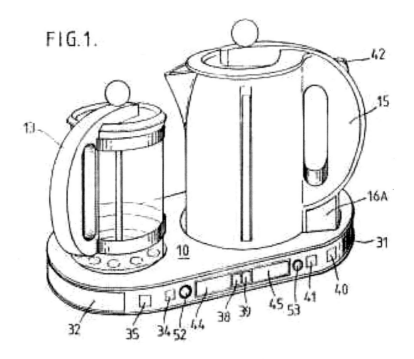

FIG. 1.

BIBLIOGRAPHY

A Working Mechanic (pseud.), *The Modern Velocipede: Its History and Construction* (G. Maddick, 1869).

Barker, Stuart, *TT Century: One Hundred Years of the Tourist Trophy* (Century, 2007).

Bradshaw, J., *Ordinary* (JRB Publishing, 2013).

Clements, Frank, *A Bike Ride Through My Life* (Trafford Publishing, 2011).

Clew, Jeff, *Vintage Motorcycles* (Shire Publications Ltd., 2009).

Dodsworth, Roger, *Glass and Glassmaking* (Shire Publications Ltd., 1982).

Ellis, J., *Glassmakers of Stourbridge and Dudley 1612–2002; A Biographical History of a Once Great Industry* (Jason Ellis, 2002).

Haden, David, *From Glass to Cycles: The Story of the Haden Family* (Lulu. com, 2006).

Haden, Sally, 'They Went to Larn 'em; How four British glassmakers played a key part in the modernisation of Japan's glass industry in the late 19th century,' *The Journal of The Glass Association*, vol. 10 (2014).

Hajdamach, Charles R., *British Glass 1800–1914* (Antique Collectors' Club, England, 1991)

Hopkins, Eric, *Birmingham; The Making of the Second City 1850–1939* (Tempus, 2001).

Inoue, Akiko, *British Influence on the Shinagawa Glassworks; Japan's First Industrial Glass Factory* (Annales du 16e Congrès de l'Association Internationale pour l'Histoire du Verre, London 2003).

Inoue, Akiko, 'Kogyosha and Shinagawa Glassworks (1); The Establishment of the First Western-style Glassworks in Japan,' *Journal of the Association for Glass Art Studies,* vol. 52, pp.10–31 vol. (2009).

Land, Nigel, *Elswick-Hopper of Barton-on-Humber; The Story of a Great British Cycle Maker* (Fathom Press, 2011).

Lumley, P., *Bicycle Trade and Industry* (Peter Lumley, 1994).

Moulton, Alex, *Alex Moulton; From Bristol to Bradford-on-Avon – A Lifetime in Engineering* (The Rolls-Royce Heritage Trust, 2009).

Shill, Ray, *Birmingham's Industrial Heritage 1900–2000* (Sutton Publishing, 2002).

Velox (pseud.), *Velocipedes, Bicycles and Tricycles* (Routledge, 1869).

INDEX